*Spirits That Come For
A Human Experience*

Order this book online at www.trafford.com/07-1055
or email orders@trafford.com

Most Trafford titles are also available at major online book retailers.

© Copyright 2007 Jamie Best.

All rights reserved. No part of this publication may be reproduced, stored in a retrieval system, or transmitted, in any form or by any means, electronic, mechanical, photocopying, recording, or otherwise, without the written prior permission of the author.

Note for Librarians: A cataloguing record for this book is available from Library and Archives Canada at www.collectionscanada.ca/amicus/index-e.html

Printed in Victoria, BC, Canada.
This book was printed on 100% recycled paper.

ISBN: 978-1-4251-2963-7

Illustrations reproduced by Inspirations. www.inspirations.uk.net
Front cover image: Nasa and The Hubble Heritage Team (STScI/AURA)

We at Trafford believe that it is the responsibility of us all, as both individuals and corporations, to make choices that are environmentally and socially sound. You, in turn, are supporting this responsible conduct each time you purchase a Trafford book, or make use of our publishing services. To find out how you are helping, please visit www.trafford.com/responsiblepublishing.html

Our mission is to efficiently provide the world's finest, most comprehensive book publishing service, enabling every author to experience success. To find out how to publish your book, your way, and have it available worldwide, visit us online at www.trafford.com/10510

Trafford PUBLISHING www.trafford.com

North America & international
toll-free: 1 888 232 4444 (USA & Canada)
phone: 250 383 6864 ♦ fax: 250 383 6804 ♦ email: info@trafford.com

The United Kingdom & Europe
phone: +44 (0)1865 722 113 ♦ local rate: 0845 230 9601
facsimile: +44 (0)1865 722 868 ♦ email: info.uk@trafford.com

10 9 8 7 6 5 4 3 2

Contents

- 4   Dedication And Declaration
- 6   Introduction
- 13   The Search For God
- 20   Saying The Same Thing

26   Part 1 – Creation

- 27   The Tao Of Creation
- 28   Exposing The Mystery
- 30   The Formation Of A Solar System
- 36   The Reality Of Our Own Solar System
- 43   The Balanced Cycle Of Energy
- 49   Planes Of Existence
- 55   The Evolution Of Individual Spirits On Earth
- 70   The Natural Cycle Of Reincarnation
- 79   The Self-regulating Nature Of Karma
- 85   Love, Light And Healing

105   Part 2 – Evolution

- 106   A Brief Insight Into Human Evolution
- 108   The Collective Mind
- 111   The Fall From Grace
- 118   The Construction Of The Abyss
- 121   The Exposure Of Christ
- 151   The Time Of Decision
- 164   The Second Coming
- 178   The Logic Of Living In The Present
- 199   Possibilities Of The Future

207   Part 3 – Self-discovery

Dedication And Declaration

This book was written as a prophecy from God, unto whom all is dedicated. But you will need to read on to truly appreciate what is meant by this, as to me prophecy is no more than speaking from the heart that which flows through naturally, without the influence of personal desires. This is not so much a form of future prediction, but more a case of outlining the path and direction of our continuing evolution; something that we are all an inseparable part of. For me prophecy is connecting with and surrendering completely to this natural and organic process of evolution, and simply giving it a voice. These words are the voice given to that experience of surrender and what has been translated and communicated.

I make no declarations in search of allegiance and belief, nor do I ask anything of you, the reader, save an open mind. What is written here is part of my fulfilment in coming into human nature, to pass on what the Universe wishes to offer, through the best words that I have been able to find. While I exist as a human being and express myself through the veil of personality, this is no longer my identity and human nature no longer offers any personal challenge. The challenge in life for me now exists in how to serve the Universe: to be carried by its energy and walk alongside the steps of others, to encourage their enlightenment. I look not to interfere or dictate, for each of us treads a unique path, I am here to support and guide and to react when ever called upon, according to the flow of consciousness.

And so this book has come to be written and is yours to take or leave as you please. It is offered as a guide, to help human beings to understand what is happening to our world in a chaotic time of transition, and, more importantly, as an encouragement for all to find their own answers and follow their own hearts. This is where our sole responsibility lies: to discover and know ourselves, and so to become in time self-realised spiritual beings, in support of all evolving life. Please do not be taken aback by this declaration of prophecy, for as you read on you will see that we are all reflections and voices of God, equally valued and serving the evolution of the Universe.

It has become my natural perception to know that I have been here before, and no doubt will come back again after this life has passed. Through these words, God, the energy and consciousness of the Universe, looks to reassure you that all is in safe hands. I do realise that while this book may help some to see more clearly, to others around the world it would be better used as kindling to light a fire for warmth, or as food to stay the hunger. Written words can only feed the mind, and how you digest these ideas is up to you and your own individual perceptions. But the time has already begun when all needs shall come to find their fulfilment, and balance shall be restored... Please read on and enjoy, for you are the medium through which this transformation takes place. That means every single human being alive, for there are no special or chosen ones in the eyes of the Universe, all are equally valued as part of creation. This is why you have come to exist...

Introduction

Like an artist mixing and stroking the paint onto a piece of canvas, or a sculptor mindfully chipping away at the clear face of rock before them, so it is that all things within the Universe are created from the original inspirations of consciousness and imagination, and are thus guided towards their aims in evolution. Could life and creation really be this simple...? While the vastness and entirety of the Universe is at present beyond our complete comprehension, could there be a singular intelligence behind it all, something that we may know and come to understand? From experience I have found that this is indeed our true reality, beyond all doubt, and I believe that through each of our individual minds we are part of that intelligence, along with everything else in the Universe. You of course may view this as a matter of personal opinion, even though it is a knowing I feel beyond personality and question. But then we each are compelled to find our own answers in order to find true certainty, for this is where our evolution now leads us.

At present all scientific measurement and theory breaks down at some point: from the smallest component of the atom to the present confines of the known and measurable Universe, at some point measurement starts to limit our thinking and becomes so large or small as to become meaningless to our day-to-day lives. As you look into the night sky and see only a tiny fraction of what is there in space, so it is within our minds that we have only come to know a tiny fraction of what we are and shall be. Beyond our present perceptions, an awareness of the true nature of God, of the infinite and eternal, awaits us all, with every soul approaching its own unique experience of birth. The scientific basis of physical perception and measurement will never be able to define eternity, for it has no common frame of reference or experience that could prove such a reality and state of being. None that is except for a conscious human being, for every mind and soul is an integral part of the Universe's self-awareness. You are an inseparable part of the mind of God. So it is that we must come to know and experience that part of ourselves, each of us as individuals, before we can then begin to relate to it and understand it, and see it in the world around us.

It is my understanding that the Universe is pulsating with life of all kinds: atoms, stars, planets and beings. Life forms and beings that lie outside of our solar system are at present beyond direct comparison, and many are even beyond the reaches of our imaginations. The human race is still very much in its early stages of self-awareness, and before we can be freed out into the rest of the Universe and its consciousness, we first must learn from experience to overcome the extremes of our primal animal instincts; defensive emotions that may lead to destructive selfishness and violence. Such uncontrollable energies would only serve to destabilise the Universe; a highly complex and interconnected structure of balance, composed of many different forms of life and states of being. And so we stand in the present, continually evolving and stepping forwards: piecing together the meandering evolution of our past, living from day-to-day through the varied practices and rituals of our many cultures and societies, toing and froing to maintain a living, and curiously peering through the opening window of our minds, to view and ponder the immensity of our Universe and understand our place within it.

So what do I have to offer through these words? What part can I play in this unique journey of awakening and self-discovery? Well I cannot give something that is yours alone to discover. I merely offer the vision of life through my eyes and the experience of my soul to date, that is yours to take or leave as you please. I have no lists of commandments or religious practices for you to follow, under the pretext that they may lead you to enlightenment. There are no rules or scripture to adhere to..., no scientific laws or facts that must be defined and believed. The only qualification required is an open mind.

And so it is that behind the faces we present to the world on a day-to-day level, the miracle of our evolution continues to take place. As you travel to work and go about your daily business, through whatever means you maintain a living and support yourself and your family, it is from behind the face, through the most intimate moments of silence within yourself, through your internal dialogue and most personal thoughts, that you grow towards complete self-discovery. All your thoughts and feelings, at this and every passing moment of time, come from a real and legitimate connection to the Universe. Regardless of how mundane or inspiring they may be, they represent your interaction with consciousness and the energy of all about you. How you choose to expose and express these thoughts and feelings is what then shapes your personality and decides how much people come to know the real you inside. How you contemplate and expand upon these instincts, thus dictates how you come to fulfil your evolution upon this Earth.

Consciousness, thought, awareness, when this is directed it becomes the source of all motion and life. This is the real and defining energy behind all existence and creation: from the Universe and all of its star systems, to your own natural breathing as you read these words, to the modern day gadgets within your home, and the substance of the bricks with which they are built..., all were created from the energy of consciousness. This is my understanding of God: as a source it is a limitless potential of conscious energy known to us as spirit, while as a being, within the framework and fabric of time and space, it is the very Universe itself: living, breathing, growing and aware, through every individual form and state of being it has created. We as human beings are just one image of this creation. We are representations of God, in our bodies, our minds and our souls.

God is an intelligence gathering energy of infinite potential, that first creates and then looks through our eyes, inspiring our thoughts and directing our every step through the impetus and directives of evolution. As such it always has purpose and direction, and these are the directives of evolution that guide our way forward. God's imagination is reflected in all you see about you on this Earth: it is the reflection you see in the mirror, the life and form of all things on this Earth, and it is the millions of stars you see in the night sky. So you see, such a God is anything but beyond our sight or reach. It is expressed in everything that you see and everything that you are, and one day you will come to know God as the life and consciousness that is your own.

What I have attempted to present in this book is a new and complete vision of the Universe, and how we as human beings are evolving within it. It represents the best words I have come to find, as of yet, to express the reality of being alive in human form, and to define some purpose and direction to this life on Earth. Do not be fooled by this statement, as I do not write to dictate to you how you should visualise the Universe, nor the concept of God you must accept, it is quite the opposite in fact. I look only to breakdown and open up all that at present restricts and dictates to our own freedom of thought and expression; you alone are left to discover your own mind and to express this in your own words.

It is my sole aim through this book to offer a natural and grounded perspective to life, that we are all in truth, **spirits that come here for a human experience**. No matter how intense, serious, or painful life may seem to become for us at times, we will always pass through and come out the other side, having grown in spirit and self-awareness, for this is the underlying priority behind our existence. I may use terms that are common to both traditional religions and science in my attempt to convey this simple vision, but I would like to make it clear that I adhere to no cult, religion or scientific theory in particular. I am writing as a simple human being, living upon this Earth today, amidst a Universe of infinite potential and imagination. While the mundane experience of living from day-to-day may occupy much of my time and shape the face of my present personality, it does not dictate the limits of my thoughts, and it is from behind this face that I now speak and truly exist as a human being.

The book is divided into three main parts, which are not meant to be conventional, so you can read in what ever manner suits your frame of mind: cover to cover, individual headings of interest, or just indiscriminate pages. The first part of the book looks to explain the simple process of creation: from the conception and opening of a star, to its evolving planets and beings, it is the transformation of consciousness and its potential energy, into atoms, light and motion, that has given us the real experience of life on Earth. The Sun is now exposed as a 'white hole', acting to transform the potential energy of original spirit and consciousness into the kinetic light radiation and motions that define life and physical existence. Each star is a white hole into time and space (as its collapsing and closing is already understood to be a black hole). They are tunnels for spirit and consciousness to enter into and manifest and experience their physical creations and beings, and in doing so spirit gains individual identity and awareness, according to its unique experience. This first part then goes on to explain the nature of a solar system in relation to our own Sun and our own evolving human nature. It describes the different levels of our consciousness in relation to the progressive planets of our solar system, the progression of our many lives and growing awareness of our individual souls, and the common human nature of love and continual intelligent communications of light.

The second part of the book focuses almost entirely upon the more recent evolution of our consciousness: the needs and directives laid down in our collective consciousness, the changing aspects and undertones of our recent history, and the effects upon us as individuals. Consciousness and evolution is shown to be fluid, acting upon our world according to need and attraction, and reacting to the challenges that arise within our nature. It describes how our instinctive priorities are being gradually transformed and superseded, from the animal priorities of fear and self-preservation, that have helped us to survive and adapt as a race, to the new Universal priorities of an open state of love and collective awareness, where we come to exist as a conscious individual soul, inseparable from the infinite mind of God. This part then goes on to examine the present nature of our societies as a reflection of this process of transformation, and how these may come to change in the future. Far from, 'losing our way', or, 'making a mess of the world', we can begin to see that the obstacles in our nature and the problems these have created, were introduced by the Universe and are part of the creative experience of human nature. The challenge for us is simply as to whether we surrender to and fully embody our nature, or whether we continue to battle with it according to our personal fears and doubts. Ultimately evolution leads us forward in a destined direction; how we walk this path and what we create and experience along the way, is the unique experience that enlightens our soul and entity. We come here for the experience of the journey and will always eventually reach our destination, even if the horizon is not yet within our vision...

The third and final part of the book is a collection of intuitive writings that represent the real and intense personal experience of my own questioning and self-discovery. As my mind looked to understand some purpose in life, and my heart ached to be free of what was imposed by social conditioning and other people's thinking, so this voice and these words came forward within me. Old perspectives and judgements were broken down and released, while new and completely original and unconditional insights naturally fell into their rightful place. The progressive projections of the mind is the experience reflected in these writings. They chronicle the disillusionment and death of my old self, and the subsequent re-birth of my soul's awareness of the Universe in this life. It is presented here as a real living example of the natural process of transformation that takes place through us all. Of course your pathway and its words will be different, but the end result will always lead us to the same place...: the heavenly state of being, that comes from discovering the knowledge and awareness of the Universe and consciously becoming the free eternal energy of spirit.

These words now belong to you. I lay down a challenge through these words, to those people who presently uphold the views of our most popular science and religion, to read and respond to what is outlined here. Not necessarily to accept or deny it, but to consider it possible, for this is after all the open minded approach and how consciousness remains creative and fluid. It is not enough for an artist to just conceive an idea, for without creation and form there is no art and no life. We must be brave enough to put pen to paper and to see where this may lead, before the picture can be made complete, to be seen and appreciated as part of creation. I hope these words may at least stimulate some thought and questioning, or go some way to being a pleasant distraction while you walk along your chosen path....

Jamie Best   1st May 2007

<u>The Search For God</u>

In each of us; there is everything

There are no real mysteries to life that cannot be known, for all that we need to know is available to us through the open doorway of the mind. As human beings, it is our nature and reason to learn and gain knowledge from the experience of life on Earth. So what have we learnt? To survive and reproduce..., to adapt to and recreate our surroundings using the Earth's natural resources..., to think, question and explore our own biology, psychology and spirituality, and that of our environment. All these instincts are given to us by the impetus of evolution; we are inseparable from the Universe and its nature, and in acceptance of this, we can begin to learn of its true nature and the direction it follows for ourselves.

There are no intellectual levels or hierarchies we must reach to discover and realise the spiritual freedom of life. Our present perception of intellect is in many cases a human judgement that creates class and division where there needn't be any. Intelligence can be sensual and intuitive as well as literate, scientific and numerate, and it is a shame that at present most measurements of the intellect are taken from how much somebody can facilitate our commercial societies, as opposed to their wholistic human qualities. It is our awareness that determines our understanding of life, and we are all equally useful as regards expanding the Universe's experience and offering a unique perspective to this magnificent creation.

So what is our awareness, and from where do we draw our identity? Are we animal, human...? Are we subject to nationality, creed, religion, personality or genetic physical traits.....? Or are we spiritual entities...? Expressions of the Universal will and intelligence incarnate in human form: a conscious, individual, and unique soul, embodied in a temporary Earthly living organism and communicating through a constructed personality?

It is my understanding that the human race is still but a child within the Universe. A child that is passing through the traumatic transition of adolescence, to eventually become a more responsible and collective being, in communion with the consciousness of the whole Universe. Our physical genetic origins lie in the Earth, in our animal nature, where selfishness dominates in the instincts to survive, reproduce and adapt. And where the balance and reason of life and death is held by nature, beyond our awareness. This is where Darwin's survival of the fittest reigns supreme: the violent act of killing is a compulsion of nature that carries no judgement of right or wrong, it is a totally natural instinct of survival. Yet our spiritual origins and core identity lie in God, in the nature, energy and consciousness of the Universe. And it is our present expansion of mind and conscience that begins to reveal this awareness to us: the collectiveness of our race, the interconnectedness of all life acting and reacting together, the providence of nature and evolution to of brought us to this point where we can question our existence, and the selfless open state of acceptance to life that is love.

Mankind has for some time been torn between these two identities: the animal nature and the God nature. We are being driven by the force of evolution to relinquish our more base and selfish desires, which is reflected in the pain of our emotions towards brutality, violence, greed and injustice. We are encouraged more to communicate and co-operate, and learn from this experience that we are stronger together and can provide more collectively. We are learning that rather than fear, a respect, tenderness and affection for each other, can breed a lasting stability, which in time can lead us to a real peace and ongoing joy of life. This growing collective relationship expands outwards to connect with everything: our immediate environment, the planet as a whole, and eventually the entire Universe.

The transition is both painful and joyful. Firstly it is painful, in the exposure of fear, in what we are forced to give up and let go of as regards our selfish animal nature, which protects and comforts, and seeks power and dominance as a form of self defence. Beyond this though it is the most joyful experience of life, in the discovery of our true origins and identity, which is gradually revealed to our awareness as we let go of old self-defence mechanisms. This alone is what leads us towards a natural peace on Earth and an appreciation for the wonder of all its life, for this can never be enforced. This freedom opens the door to the Universe and the infinite potentials that await, and it continues to deliver fulfilment to our own evolution and being. It is our spiritual genetic progression.

As you can see by the world we live in and the societies we have created, we are still fairly primitive and have some way to go to actually realise the paradise we are potentially born into. But I have no doubt that the force of evolution that is responsible for our existence, will in time see us through. It compels us to grow up, to change and move forward, and try as we (or our fearing animal nature) might, we cannot resist it. At times I have been aware of a strong sense of guilt within the human race, that we have gone wrong somewhere or lost our way and 'offended God'. But we need to accept this is the way we have chosen and the path we are now walking if we are to gain an awareness of the Universe and discover and realise our true spiritual identity. As we learn from experience, then often we choose to learn things the hard and painful way, going round in circles until we realise our mistakes. But this only means that the lessons we learn become that much more certified and inherent within us. All experience is a progression in life, and as our conscience naturally grows both individually and collectively, as we accept to take more responsibility for our actions, so we edge towards the equality, prosperity and peace, that may truly unleash our creative potential.

The world is the way it is, we cannot change the past we can only accept it. In doing so we can open our eyes to the present, take life back into our hands and be truly honest about the present ways of our world, to give ourselves the freedom to evolve naturally. It is common sense when you stop to think, but a lesson that we have been learning for many centuries now: to fight against our nature and its evolution, is to cut off the hand that feeds us with life, which can only eventually lead to experiences of self-destruction... Sometime in the future we will realise this as a race, and so be free to move on again.

As human beings we have naturally come to question our consciousness and search for a power and origin to our existence. It is a quest to find identity and some deeper meaning and purpose to our lives. These instincts have led us to elaborate creation myths, build and structure mass religions and belief systems, explore numerous directions in metaphysics and philosophical doctrines, and scientifically measure and ponder the very size and substance of creation and the original creative act. From our present perspective it may seem at times like a battle, a struggle that offers no guarantees, with the way ahead dark, fearful and unknown. But try to see it from the other side, from the perspective of the evolving Universe: every revelation and discovery we make, is just the natural tide of the Universe, opening and realising what is already our potential human nature and awareness. We as open and sensitive human beings merely contact and expose this unfolding; we are all channels and earths to this flow of energy, expressing it through our unique personality. As such we need not fear, but merely follow and live by our true nature and instincts and the rest will unfold before us.

Everything works according to a balance of energy that flows like a current, directed by the polarity of need and attraction. Where there is need within us then energy and its experience is attracted to us and we are encouraged to seek it out. While as an open channel, that is connected to a need outside of its immediate self (to heal or support growth), so energy can flow through and we are attracted to the need or it is drawn to us. Thus is everything in the Universe born and created through the motion and interaction of positive and negative states of energy, and its polarity of need and attraction that seeks to restore balance and harmony.

The difficulties and conflicts only arise in human nature when the opinions and ideologies of one person are used to try and dominate the freethinking, discovery, and expression of others. This will never fulfil or satisfy the individual need for self-discovery and truth that is a condition of our nature and evolution. Only through the profound experience of finding our own answers to our own questions can we ever find certainty, and from this, peace and stability. If there is a common origin to our spirit and human nature, a fact of which I have absolutely no doubt, then we will only ever freely come to recognise this and find unity in it, if we are to discover and experience it for ourselves, and are free to express it through our own unique individuality. This common experience of self-realisation is the only way we can come together in freedom; it is the unique pathway our lives carve out as they meander their way towards God.

God is just a simple three-letter word, the one that we have formed and chosen to convey the concept of a creator and guiding intelligence to our existence. Any human can claim they speak for God in the words or images they portray, but if these in any way inhibit or dictate to our own free will or free expression, then the voice behind them is that part of our animal nature that fears exposure and rejection to the extreme that it feels it must compensate, and it does so by seeking to control and dictate the thinking of others. Again we seem to be learning many of our lessons the hard way, but learn we must, for evolution demands it. We have come to clothe God in the many different images of our cultures and ideologies in an attempt to personify nature and the Universe, and personalise our relationship with them. All types of religion (tribal, shamanism, traditional, cultism, even Satanism and atheism, to name a few) expose a common need in mankind to develop his belief in and understanding of creation. Science also springs from the same curiosity and instinct. None of course actually dictate how the Universe and evolution unfolds, nor do they define the nature of God; they are our personal representations of God and not singularly how God represents itself. They do all however have something genuine to say about our human nature and the levels of our awareness, and an unbiased anthropological view of these can be very revealing as to the present focus and intent of our evolution.

We all live our lives by religion, but the true religion I speak of is simply defined by our human nature: every thought, feeling and action of our day-to-day lives. No matter how alone we may feel with our thoughts at times, everything that passes through us forms an imprint in the experience of the Universe. From the most mundane to the sublime, it becomes eternal, it will always have been. Individually this creates our entity and becomes our enlightenment, our soul, and this realisation itself is a form of liberation: if nothing remains hidden from the Universe, then what reason do we have to hide anything of ourselves or our nature. So called enlightenment is simplicity itself, it is the simple acceptance of ourselves, to live completely by our nature and express it to the full, for in reality we can do or be nothing else. Regardless of our present personal allegiance to whatever man-made religion or ideology, and aside from whatever image we may create or project about ourselves, which may or may not serve us for the present, the truth of our religion is exposed in the reality of our entire human experience and the paths that we walk throughout life. What we aspire to and strive for in life, is what we have then come to worship.

If the purpose of evolution is to create a diversity of life and beings, to experience an expansive range of perspectives to life and to develop new thoughts and ideas from these insights, then it has always had perfection in its aim, and we are but one of the eyes that it evolves and looks through. There are no norms or standards that we must configure to, no singularly perfect human being we all must aim to be. We are each ourselves, our own original entity of experience, and every soul that ever comes to be upon this Earth, lives by its own unique life force and religion. This realisation will, in time, bring the awareness of God into every aspect of our day-to-day lives;

God has always been there, it is just a case of when we realise how natural and ordinary it is....

Saying The Same Thing

Language is just a framework of differing cultural constructions, while the spirit that gives it life and meaning, is universal.

In our present small bracket of time we have the two mainstream mediums of science and traditional religion at our disposal. These are presently the most common approaches to questioning our existence and explaining the structure and meaning of life and the Universe. Each have their own unique approach and language:

Science professes itself to be the fixed or factual approach. Its direction of questioning and the laws and ideas it perpetuates, rely almost entirely upon the proof of the physical senses, thus denying the reality (and sometimes even the possibility) of anything that lies beyond these limits of measure. Scientific law and understanding is developed through a combination of personal theory, hypothesis, observation and experimentation. The extreme of the scientific view, believes that man has evolved purely by chance and has the complete free will to do as he pleases: everything is governed by physical laws, that once understood and mastered, can be used to manipulate and recreate our environment according to our desired tastes, and in many cases of recent times, regardless of the impact to our natural environment.

Traditional religion offers a more metaphysical and intuitive approach, which aspires to the spiritual sense of being. Most of the established religions are ritualised: built around the words and experiences of past human beings, that have since been elevated to the status of saints or gods, according to their outstanding abilities and beliefs. Many of the extreme religious views and orders, dictate that we must give up our free will and bow down to a being greater than we may ever come to know. We must follow the laws and teachings and the unquestionable will of their particular church (its dogma and its leaders) and in doing so we may eventually reap the professed rewards of their particular Heaven. They advise us to deny the temptation of anything that conflicts with their teachings, and in some cases to try to convert those who do not agree with their beliefs (as if this is the only way for a soul to be 'saved' or enlightened).

These are the two very basic extremes, with most beliefs lying somewhere fused or confused between the two. As these institutions have evolved with us other many centuries, in many cases they seem to have become viewed as an end in themselves, and we are taught or educated more to be at their disposal. There are many truths and there is much to learn about our history, psychology and approach to life, within these institutions, but they are merely individual and collective mediums towards our further understanding of creation. They are concepts and images of representation rather than singularly defined truths, and on their own, without human spirit or voice, they are empty vessels: frameworks of differing constructions.

At their extremes, these two approaches claim to be separate from and more righteous than the other, and yet they both expose exactly the same need and instinct within mankind, namely the desire to form and express a deeper understanding of nature and of our relationship with creation. As with all extremes, if we give ourselves only to one side, then we may become ignorant to the value of the other. And so the battle between science and religion is fuelled only by the arrogant and forceful opinions of those who stand on either side and the numbers of their followers. It has become a battle for power over peoples' lives and thinking, another remnant of our fearing animal nature that seeks to dominate, and it is a fight that will only ever come to an end when we decide to give up fighting each other and work together. If we choose to give up our instinct of freethinking and take our beliefs from something that lies outside of our own heart, then no matter how subtly its chains are concealed, we become obligated and have given ourselves to slavery. This arrogance in man, that the concept of belief in one should be so righteous as to dominate and crush that of another, is at the very root of most of our wars and destructive tendencies. Yet it is the continual revolutionary reaction towards this repression, that helps to expose and strengthen our natural evolutionary compulsion towards the freedom of thought and expression for every individual; only this will enable true self-realisation. Again we seem to be learning our lessons the hard way, but the compulsive instinct towards the freedom of spirit within each of us, will always react to and overcome repression, we only need to look through the pages of our more recent history to appreciate this.

As with all things, I believe the truth lies in the balance and in our own personal experience; being open to all sides and voices, but being dependent upon and restricted by none. The two extremes combined, speak of a more simple and natural truth: mankind is formed of a higher state of being and non-manifest energy potential (spirit), that comes to Earth within temporal physical boundaries and laws (through the genetics of a human being), to individually experience creation and develop and realise its potential to become a unique spiritual entity. The higher-self is the spiritual being and energy of enlightened experience and future potential, while the lower-self is the physical being and personality developed in any one lifetime. The two come together as a human being, inseparable from each other while we live out that lifetime, and then the spirit moves on until the next incarnation. Mankind is subject to and compelled by the higher nature and directives of his evolution, but is free to create, follow and experience any path within that nature, according to personal taste and his needs to learn and evolve.

It has become the self-acclaimed authority of some scientists and religious leaders to dictate beliefs and philosophies for life, which now reflect in our politics, education systems and social morality. People often listen to and follow those who speak out the loudest or with the greatest conviction, for it can put-off having to take full responsibility for ourselves. Both extremes have laid down laws and rituals that can deny us the absolute freedom to follow the nature of our own hearts, and to make our own discoveries. In many ways our freedom is taken soon after birth, before we have the chance to express it and put it to its most creative use. We are educated with the beliefs and opinions of others: told what is good and bad, right and wrong, when our own conscience needs to be allowed to develop and trusted to reach its own conclusions. Rarely as a child are we given enough freedom and confidence to learn and discover things for ourselves, which only causes problems further down the line, as we are forced to reassess beliefs in the natural compulsion to develop our own. It is our responsibility alone to acknowledge and take back our freedom; the only substance and sustenance to the more destructive extremes of science and religion, is the spirit that we give to them or allow them to take. We will only ever naturally come together and work together as a race, through the unconditional freedom of thought and expression. This alone will allow evolution to carry us beyond and transcend our more fearing and destructive animal instincts.

The more destructive extremes of science and traditional religion, do not remain with us to further our understanding of creation and our relationship with the Universe, for this is done through the free spirit of our day-to-day lives, and through the unopposed contemplation's of an open mind. These attitudes remain with us today as a reflection of the extremities our ignorance may come to represent. They are an expose of the horrific realities of death and destruction we have put upon ourselves and our planet. The painful experience of which will help to teach us a lesson of responsibility, that will eventually open the door to the infinite creative energy of our Universe..., once we have truly learned and grown up.

As I continue in this book to trace my own path of understanding as to how and why the Universe creates matter and individual beings, and the different levels of awareness this involves, so I may come to use many different scientific and religious terms. I commit to no school of thought in particular, and use these terms merely as tools; it is only the general feeling of ideas and concepts that I am trying to convey, in a simple and available way. Although what I have written may become categorised in time, I have no intention of establishing another separate school of thought or religious ideal. Instead I aim to bring together all that is true and positive within science and religion, to unite them in their humanitarian origins. My main considered intention in writing this, is to demonstrate the simplicity of free thinking and what it can produce, for all of the ideas contained herein have come from a simple open mind, inseparably linked to the Universe as all living things are.

*Our true religion is expressed through the paths that
we walk in life;
each step forward is a new creation:
we are born into the light,
free to breathe the air,
to take in and give out of our soul:
the teachings of life come only from experience,
for it is only our fear to live, that denies us
fulfilment.*

*****

*To soar in the joys of freedom,
you must first to have been a prisoner.....*

*what are the chains that tie you down?
and how shall you come to fly?*

Part One

Creation

The Tao Of Creation

The Tao is an ancient Chinese word that seeks to define the nature and movement of all energy in creation. It describes the interconnected flow of all spirit: flowing through all substance and matter, it is the eternal wave of life that carries everything along its path in evolution. It is the path that we all walk in life, a path that has no real boundaries, save the temporal physical limitations we chose to enter through incarnation. There are no rituals but that which is the nature and expression of our being, and it has no teachings but that which we breathe and experience throughout our many lives. The Tao is not just a word, it is life itself: it is the continual ebb and flow of energy and spirit through creation and destruction that gives us our existence and awareness.

Words could never fully express its beauty and its nature, for there is no single mind or concept that could ever truly encapsulate eternity..., it just is. The only true relationship we may find to the force and direction of our creation, comes through the sensual nature of our inner-being, through the rhythmic breathing of heart and soul. It is here where the marriage begins with all that is creation, and only when we walk our way through life from the very essence and nature of our soul, to allow our heart to direct and guide, above all outside influences, does consciousness become one with the Tao..., to walk forward in purest freedom...

Exposing The Mystery

*The mystery of creation lies beyond the veil of darkness we know as fear;
if we are not brave enough to step forward into the unknown,
then how can we expect to pass through, and gain knowledge of the truth.*

A puzzle can be as simple or as complex as we make it out to be: there may only be a few pieces, so that a child could put it together within seconds, or there may be billions of pieces, so that many people would have to specialise in different areas, over many generations, to bring together a solution. This is where our relationship with life and the Universe stands: there are many theories and many pieces, with people working in highly specialised areas, hoping to gain a glimpse of the true nature and reason of the Universe, and yet this whole reality is entirely a puzzle of our own making. While we have learnt an immense amount from both religion and science, as to our nature and the mechanics of the Universe, none of this has ever changed the nature and reality of the living Universe. It is one interrelated whole, with all aspects drawn from a singular infinite energy source. There are no real pieces, it is only our nature and awareness of creation that lies in pieces.

All human evolution and conscious discovery is essentially impulsive and intuitive: the passage of our higher spiritual potential down to our conscious being upon the Earth, and out into the mental concepts and intuitive knowledge we create and project. The whole time, before, during and after our discoveries, the Universe continues in its natural order. We have never been responsible for the burning of the Sun or the revolving of the Earth. We are not in control of how it works or why it is, for in reality it has always been the other way around. Creation, the Universe, God, this has given us everything we have come to know, and only when it had deemed us ready; it breathes and evolves as naturally through us, as it does through everything else.

What follows is my own exploration into the mind of God; an understanding of how the simple re-cycling motion of energy forms the structure and framework of our particular solar system, from which we gain our physical experience and spiritual enlightenment. All forms of matter and separate states of being evolve from what was originally spirit, or potential energy, and all become channels for new spirit to gain real experience and identity. From the smallest of atoms to the largest of all star systems, the basic motions and principles of formation are the same. The original potential energy is divided into the positive and negative states that set up the framework of time and space and stimulate the motion that enables a transformation of potential to kinetic energy. The potential energy is drawn in and concentrated about a central nucleus, which transforms the potential into a kinetic radiance of light energy, and this then radiates outwards to fill the void left by the original potential energy. The nucleus and its light energy then draws in, creates, structures and manifests the desired physical beings or the environment in which to bring about those beings: elements, stars, galaxies, planets, moons, minerals, vegetation, animals, humans, anything and everything that is physically real.

Of course from the perspective of our time frames (which are purely relative to our life-span and how the Earth revolves around the Sun), this process of evolution and manifestation may take billions of years, and become a complex interconnected web of atoms, planets, life forms and ecosystems. But the cycle of creation relies on the simple relationship between potential and kinetic states of energy, and the balance of their light and dark states. Hopefully the example that follows will give this idea some definition and clarity....

The Formation Of A Solar System
Before The Beginning

In origin, before the temporal fabric of time and space is set up to enable the manifestation of a solar system, before the big bang or the divine act of creation, there is only the singular state: an infinite sea of potential energy, that is the motionless and undivided spirit. This is God as the creative source, from which everything originates. Anything and everything is possible, realities that are way beyond our present imaginations as humans, but as there is no motion, substance, or physical distinction, then nothing is actually real. It is all one conscious energy....., and I know that it is conscious, because its consciousness is reflected in every tiny detail of our creation, something that we can all relate to and communicate with through our own conscious minds.

This energy is like an infinite ocean of still and silent water that has no boundaries and pervades everything: it is the Great Spirit. Such a body of water is composed of unlimited droplets, which are potentially the individual spirits, but as there is no separation between them, the ocean remains as one whole, a singularity. If one droplet was to be given the illusory experience of separation, to create a bubble within the temporal fabric of time and space, to be turned in upon itself and to flow into the creation and experience of different environments, forms and states of being..., then it could develop its own entity. Through the open structure of its created forms (solar systems, planets, and beings) it could enable new spirit to flow through and gain experience of the cycle, to develop their own entity. The individual spirits, or entities, are still droplets encompassed within the ocean, they are always an inseparable part of it..., only now they have the self-awareness to direct, shape and support the potential of new creations and spirit to come into being. And so continues the cycle of creation within the Universe, where billions of stars are seeded.

The nature of eternity, or infinity, is impossible to define within the boundaries of a single idea or concept, it can only be touched, experienced and known through an open mind. Infinity has no boundaries and no limitations..., it just is, always has been and always will be. Anything that has a point of beginning to its existence, once had no reality and will always come to an end at some point. To be eternal there can be no beginning and no ending, the two points are one, a constant, energy... Energy cannot be created or destroyed, it can only change its form. And these changing forms represent the reality of creation in the entire Universe. Energy is God and God is energy, and everything that we are is a projection of this. Our own minds and thoughts are composed of the same creative source of energy that has created the living Universe, it is conscious and imaginative. It is hard for us to relate to energy as infinite, as we only ever express and measure it as a quantity, but such a relationship and understanding only comes through a direct and personal conscious union with the mind of God; the completion of a cycle towards which evolution leads us all, for here we come to realise our true identity and origin.

The Beginning

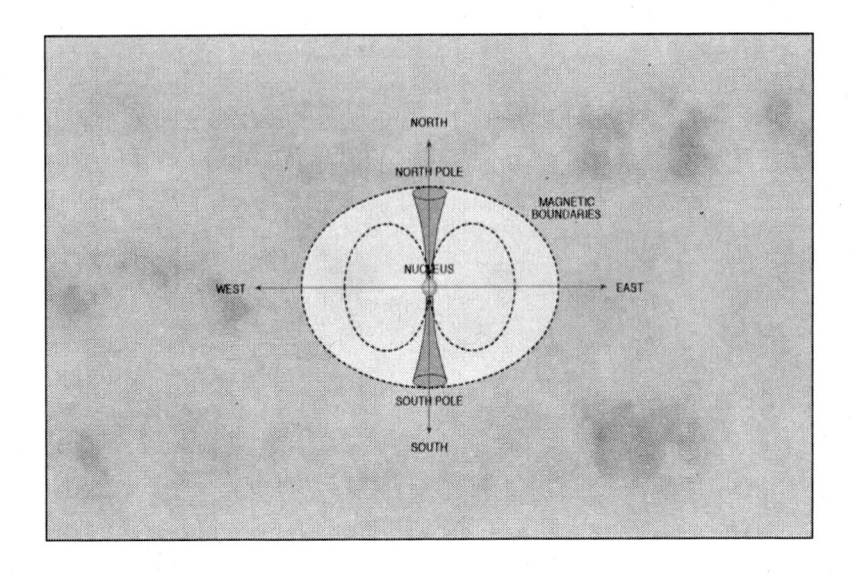

The creation of a solar system begins with the division of balanced and motionless energy into the positive and negative states that establish the framework of time and space. It is initiated according to the creative will of the infinite conscious energy of God, and the gathered intelligence of its creative experience. The division creates opposing polarities that are drawn apart about the central point, or nucleus, and as the poles separate so a magnetic field is formed about the nucleus. As this field increases, so the solar boundaries establish some stability and enable the formation of a three dimensional space within: the three dimensional planes of North, South, East and West are created and span from the central co-ordinates of the nucleus.

Time and space are the definitive co-ordinates to our temporal physical existence: our individual soul awareness incarnates into its chosen form, experiences life, and exists within an exact time and space that nothing else can truly occupy. In essence, time is the energy of motion (or motion of energy) and is purely relative. Time is the positive concentration of energy, which flows from the central nucleus as the kinetic radiance of light, and as such it is the source of all motion. Hence we have come to measure time relative to the most consistent motions around us. Space is the medium through which motion can take place and exist: space is the original negative void of energy left about the positive concentration of the nucleus, and as such it is the area in which we come to exist. All physical existence, or life as we know it, is this motion of positive energy within the negative void of space. All thoughts, feelings, experiences and actions are eternally imprinted within the collective mind of the Universe, according to their moment of reality: their distinct co-ordinate within time and space. This is how each unique entity gains its self-awareness and evolves.

Time and space are inseparable from each other, they determine each other, they are the two energy states of one originally balanced and motionless potential energy. Once divided, they interfuse in the impulse to restore balance: the energy void of space draws in, in a need to be filled, while the concentrated energy of light radiates outwards to fill space. It is this cycle and recycling of energy that enables all creation to exist and evolve in continuous motion.

The Vortices

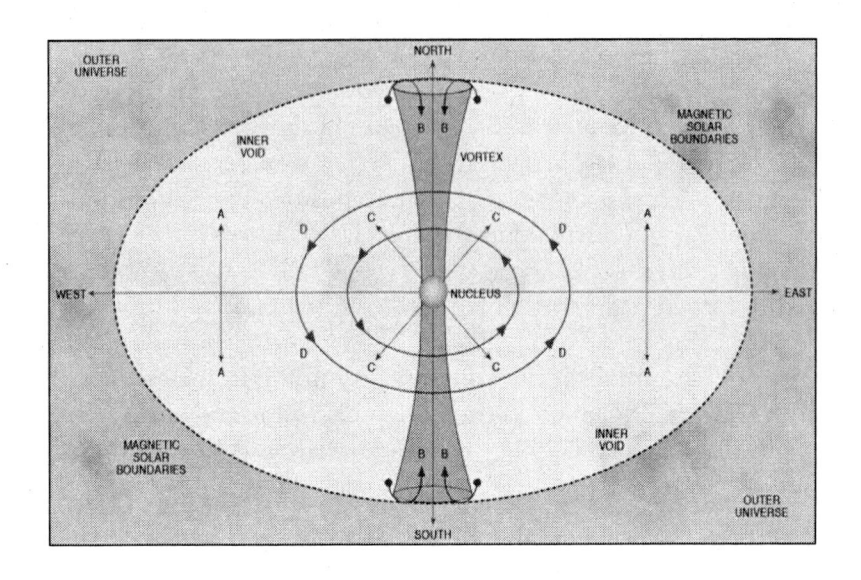

A - balanced energy drawn apart by the opposing polarities
B - energy potential drawn in and accelerated down through vortices
C - outward radiant force of light
D - motion of induced current

    As the poles are drawn apart from the central nucleus, so the potential energy within the solar boundaries of the magnetic field is drawn in at the opening vortices of the poles. It is accelerated and stepped down through the vortices to form the different potential planes of the solar system, which encapsulate the nucleus core as energy fields, like the layers of an onion. These are the spiritual seeds to the formation of all evolving matter within this star system, and at the central nucleus, the concentrated potential is made real and transformed into the kinetic radiance of light. This whole process of creating with energy, by drawing apart opposing polarities to manifest consciousness, is something that humans can learn to mediate as they evolve into a Universal awareness and state of being.

Through the nucleus, all of the original potential spirit can be transformed and made real: the energy light waves actually carry the spiritual seeds out into three dimensional space, drawing together particles and elements passed on from previous star systems. The light then actively builds and structures the original blue print formed in the planes of the vortices; travelling as waves and building as particles. The magnetic field induces a current of motion about the nucleus, and all evolving matter and life forms come to establish a stable orbit within that current.

The whole process of solar formation is as one continual movement and flow, with all levels completely interactive and interdependent. The star system and its planets and life forms, all evolve in a naturally open state of being, connected to source and continually interacting with the rest of the evolving Universe. In this respect creation is an organism that has consciousness and feeling on every level, and is open and adaptable as opposed to being purely mechanical. At any time, according to the Universal will and a solar system's creative needs, changes and new ideas can be drawn in and imprinted within the planes of the vortices, and thus eventually come to manifest within the star system. This describes a solar system as a being of feeling and awareness that is continually learning and developing new ideas and implementing them, both from the experience of its own expansion and evolution, as well as from that of the rest of the evolving Universe. It is one system working together on every level.

36

The Reality Of Our Own Solar System

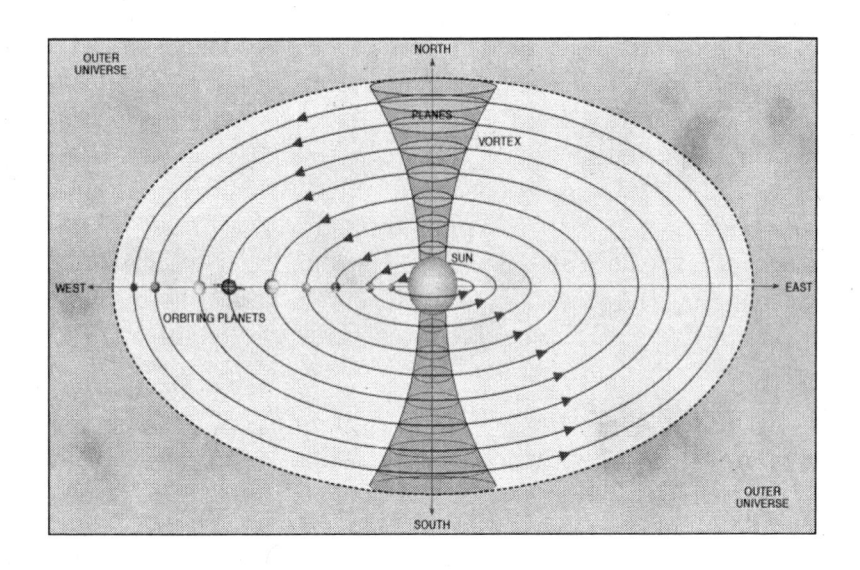

Angled/Plan View:
(some orbits are elliptical, or irregular)

Image credit: nasa.gov

Side View:
(not to scale)

Image credit: nasa.gov

In the origins of our own solar system our nucleus is more commonly referred to as the Sun, which is very similar in its nature to many of the millions of stars you might see in the night sky. The direction and nature of all the planetary evolution within our solar system is determined by the light radiation of the Sun: the basic elemental and atomic building blocks are both drawn in from matter already within the Universe (passed on from the remnants of previous solar systems), and created directly from the energy of the Sun. The basic formation of all matter is similar, from atoms to stars. If you were able to view an atom on the same scale as a solar system, then you would see that their basic structures are almost identical (a central nucleus orbited by planets or electrons). The foundations of a physical creation are composed according to the different types of relationships between atoms: attracting, building, repelling and disintegrating. The structure and formation of all matter, from a planet to a human body, are types of atomic relationships between elements and compounds, evolved together over vast time periods. They have reason and purpose to their complex natures, and all are channels for the radiation of energy and the individual experiences and enlightenment of the spirit.

This energy of spirit represents a fifth dimension, which completes the definition of our existence. We have already defined creation as the inseparable combination of three-dimensional space and the forth dimension of time..., but also inseparable from this and integral to our definition of existence, is conscious spiritual energy or awareness. Without this fifth dimensional aspect, which creates and pervades everything, then matter within space would be an empty shell and time purely a mechanical motion.

The fifth dimension of spirit is the missing link in science. It can be subdivided into many other dimensions and levels of awareness, all of which lie beyond the measurable dimensions of time and space, and the observations of our five physical senses. It is therefore something that the scientist (or any human being for that matter) can only ever come to appreciate through the realisation and experience of their own soul and spirit, and its inseparable connection to all other spirit.

Admittedly spirit does for many seem to be an extremely vague and general term, and for an ordered scientific structure of mind it can be frustrating and hard to accept: how can it be categorised and defined by law or equation...? Well the truth is, it specifically defines the central identity and source of our nature, which comes from something eternal and infinite, an energy that pervades and creates all things. Because of this, it can never be known, categorised or measured, beyond our personal and direct experience of soul and consciousness.

If we join these dimensions together, then we now have the complete co-ordinates and definition of any form of temporal creation (from an atom, to a human being, and on to our entire Universe..., where ever there is a form of identity between the microcosm and the macrocosm): we exist through matter within three dimensional space, which exists and radiates according to a relative motion of time, both of which originate from and are filled and encompassed by the energy and entity of spiritual consciousness and awareness. This gives us the complete cycle of a fifth-dimensional continuum (with the ability to subdivide dimensions within the fifth dimension), the space-time-spirit continuum.

When a solar system has built, created and evolved the physical nature and beings of the original potential blue print contained within its vortices, then it stabilises, with the positive and negative energies reaching a natural balance. The vortices are now open holes into time and space, with the solar system offering the experience of its unique nature and creation to the rest of the evolved Universe and to the further evolution of new spiritual entities. The vortices in a sense become a tunnel, directing spirit into and through the complete cycle of its unique evolution; passing on all the lessons it has learnt and all the new ideas and perspectives it has created, so that the experience and knowledge may become universally inherent. This is the most simplified reason and purpose of creation, that through the temporal physical experience of growth and evolution, individual spirits may develop their own entity and awareness, to go on to become new openings and guides to new creations within the Universe, and to help to support and adapt those already developing.

This whole cycle can easily be visualised and compared to the growth cycle of a plant or flower: a seed is planted within the darkness of the earth and fed with all the light energy, nutrients and water it needs to grow. Slowly it grows up through the earth, breaks through the soil into the light and grows into the full potential of its genetic seed. The flower then opens out to shine of the fullness of its experience. It releases many new seeds each of which contain the genetic foundations of its own particular experience of growth, and each of which may then be introduced into new soil, to experience a new path of growth, and in turn to bring forward new seeds... It is in reality a universal genetic progression, both physically and spiritually. Stars are the original seeds that then flower to create a whole galaxy of seeds; each of which evolves as a new star, which may then in turn flower and bring forth new seeds...; and so continues this wonderful Universe of creation.

No star is created in complete isolation; its solar boundaries are not distinctly marked cut-off points, but gradually merge into the rest of the Universe as the magnetic field of the nucleus gets weaker. A solar system's originating inner void draws in matter and energy from the outer Universe (passed on from previous star systems), and in this respect it is always connected to the rest of the evolved Universe (the previous diagrams are just simple illustrations of how a solar system opens and stabilises). So when I use the term void, I am not referring to an absolute void, but a negative balance of energy.

There are many different types of stars that we have come to categorise at different stages of their life-cycles (solar stars, double stars, variable stars, neutron stars..., to name but a few), but in the same way that all human beings are individual, so all stars are unique. The basic life-cycle of a star follows a general pattern: they are born of a conscious energy potential...., they come to establish their nucleus within space to radiate the kinetic energy of light (within dark and luminous nebulas)..., they then pass through a 'main sequence' period where stability is achieved and evolution takes place..., and finally they contract and disintegrate as planetary nebula, burning out white dwarfs, and novae and supernovae.

After a solar system has developed and experienced its full diversity and potential, and has passed through all possible new spirits so that the knowledge of its experience has become universally inherent, the nucleus eventually collapses in upon itself and the hole is closed up, as there is no longer a need to keep it alive. All of the remaining matter and energy within the solar system is passed on in other forms to the rest of the evolving Universe, and there are many ways that this can take place:

At one extreme, new spirit and energy is continually introduced into an evolved solar system, and there is an increase in and build up of positive energy. As the star collapses there is a massive explosion of energy out into the Universe, known as novae or supernovae, which can then be used in other creations, while the hole of this system is closed. Some stars pulse energy through the vortices and out into the Universe at regular intervals, some slowly expand outwards, diminish and burn out, and some go out in a singular fantastic explosion of energy..... At the other extreme, the nucleus may be unable to sustain its stability and existence, and pass any more new spirit through. Again it would collapse in upon itself and create what is known to us as a black hole. Here all energy and matter is drawn back into the hole and dissolved and radiated as other forms of energy. Again the hole eventually closes and balance is restored.

In this respect the birth and radiance of a star would be better understood as a white hole, whereas its death and withdrawal is sometimes exposed as a black hole. Both are holes in the sense that they represent a two-way door, through which potential energy can become a kinetic reality, and matter and light can be drawn back in and recycled in other forms or energy. There are many variations between these two extremes, but all forms of matter eventually disintegrate and pass on their energy to new forms; a solar system will only be withdrawn from existence once every last ounce of potential has been passed through and its knowledge and experience has become Universally inherent. Nothing is ever lost or ever truly dies, as the energy and spirit of creation is eternal. It is a simple and natural recycling of energy that continues to amass the intelligence of experience; to develop new ideas and potential, and then bring them into creation as new star systems.

Of course the question remains at the end of all this as to whether the Universe had an actual point of origin or creation: with an infinite source and infinite potential for creations, has the Universe been in a continual cycle of solar formation and disintegration..., or was there actually a beginning point to it all, an original conscious creative act? This I feel is not a question that our limited rational minds will ever be able to contain and answer. Again this answer lies in the experience of our eternal nature and identity, for within this experience what we perceive as physically real in our present personalities and their rational thinking, becomes exposed as just a temporary state of being and passing experience. As our consciousness merges and exists in communion with the infinite mind of God, so all realities are exposed and our minds no longer think in terms of beginnings and endings. They are eternal, part of the continuum, and they come to feel the infinite cycle of creation and destruction exposed by the Universe as part of that eternity.

The Balanced Cycle Of Energy

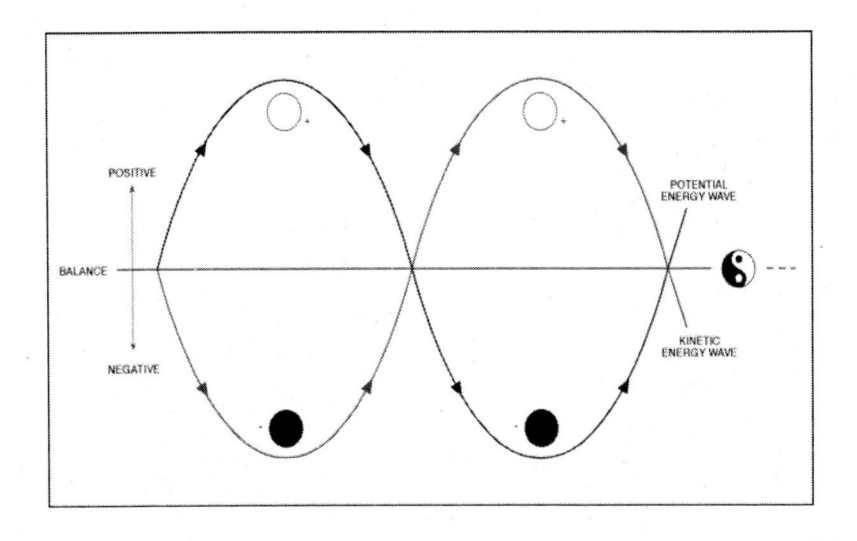

The central line represents the Universal source of creation, the infinite, balanced and motionless energy potential..., and the symbol along side is the Taoist symbol for the continual motion and interaction of light and dark (time and space, positive and negative, yang and yin, masculine and feminine) that is the nature of the living Universe. This line in no way represents any time scale, as this is relative to each unique creation, it merely exposes the opposing balance of potential and kinetic states of energy: what ever is drawn out kinetically, first originated as potential spirit. While the individual nature of all stars differs, there are four main stages to the wave cycle of energy, which is representative of the life cycle of a solar system: separation, growth, radiance and disintegration. The flow of energy is similar to that in an electric current, with the current direction flowing from negative to positive or positive to negative, according to the perspective of which energy wave you follow (a negative balance of energy represents a void, while a positive balance represents light). The two energy waves move along in unison as they represent the two energy states of one original source. The more potential that is brought to light, the more kinetic work is done and the more creation becomes a living physical reality.

The Four Kinetic Stages Of The Cycle

Following the kinetic wave of energy, this is what you would see as physically real, as regards the motion, creation and life span of a solar system.

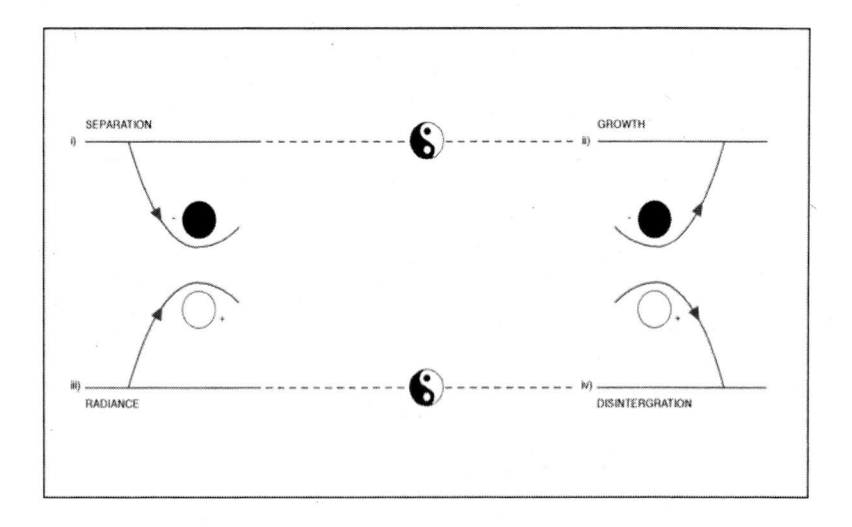

i) **Separation**:- the first part of the motion sees the separation of energy into positive and negative states, which creates the mediums of the positive forward motion of time and the negative three dimensional void of space. The central co-ordinate of the star draws in the potential energy to create its nucleus, which in turn draws in matter (gas and dust) from the surrounding area, passed on from previous star systems. This forms a nebula within which the star system can begin to form and evolve, a kind of cocoon that enables the star to stabilise and establish its boundaries, whilst feeding it with the substance it needs to build.

ii) **Growth**:- the second part of the motion represents the construction and evolution of different physical forms and beings, such as planets, elements, minerals, vegetation and animals. This creative experience is completed when the wave reaches the central 'still point'. Here the original positive and negative energies find a balance, and the solar system becomes fully stabilised and open to the rest of the evolved Universe and to the entry of new spiritual entities.

iii) **Radiance**:- the third part of the motion draws in more potential energy by introducing and evolving new individual spirits into its unique creation. Here the solar system opens, radiates and passes through further positive energy, as well as interacting with other beings and star systems, which adds to and continues the experience and creation of its own reality.

iv) **Disintegration**:- the final part of the motion sees the collapse of the star system and the passing on of all of its energy and experience in the form of gases, basic elements, energy waves, and in the enlightened spiritual entities that may support new creations. As the waves meet the central line a balanced and motionless singular state is restored, the hole is closed and the solar system no longer exists as a physical reality.

This whole process of solar creation works in a similar way to a lung, breathing in and out through the vortices and central nucleus. Potential energy or spirit is breathed in through the vortices and transformed through the nucleus into kinetic energy and light radiation, which fills the inner void with life and animation. This is then breathed out as new spiritual entities and as novae and supernovae (along with other energy radiations), to share with the rest of the Universe and to help form the foundations of new creations and star systems. This is a very simplistic view of what is a highly complex and delicately poised reality, but it serves to expose the basic nature and reasoning behind creation.

It is through our own forms of artistic creation (painting, sculpting, writing, singing, dancing, etc.), that we most naturally learn about and understand the archetypal nature of the creative Universe. In everything that we create, even our daily routines and personalities, we are channels for the creative impulse of the Universe, using the elements and images of our environment and the intuitive nature of our soul. In fact if we go on to compare the two, then this reflection offers a clear comparison as to the nature of the Universe and how this is expressed in our own creativity:

In the beginning there is the void, empty and lifeless : which is the artist's canvas, completely clear and void of materials, shape and form. Then there is the conscious spiritual potential for creation, that would bring life, form and being throughout the void : which is the inspiration of the artist, the impulse and idea within heart and mind. As the light energy shines throughout the void to create form and structure, so the potential is made real in the form of a living breathing star system : in the same way that thought and feeling take shape through the motion of the artist's pen or brush, transferring his imagination into a physical reality. As the artist creates his or her picture they are open and adaptable, their ideas may change and expand and follow new paths as they learn from and interact with what they are creating : so it is with a star system, which is continually open and interacting with its original intelligent source and the rest of the evolving Universe. When a star system's construction is complete, then it openly radiates of the entire knowledge and experience that went into it : just as a finished piece of art is displayed for all to see, appreciate and learn from. Eventually the reality and experience of a star system becomes Universally inherent and its form is dissolved, with the energy being passed on to new creations : as with a piece of art that no longer has anything to offer or teach mankind that is taken from its place of display; the canvas, frame, and paints can be used again, recycled to be used in whatever way is appropriate for something new to be created. This continual recycling is a very important part of the nature of the Universe, a lesson that we are just beginning to learn and appreciate here on Earth.

All things in creation are forms of art, radiating life and spirit. They are receptacles and carriers of energy, channels through which spirit can gain awareness and experience, the temporary vehicles of a physical existence. Every type of human art and creativity exposes the nature of spiritual expression; we are all artists, even in our personalities and day-to-day lives, no one is any greater than another, just different. If you could imagine your deepest and most passionate feelings created into a form that you could touch and embrace, even enter into, embody and communicate through, then you can touch upon the very reason for creation. And it is in the experience of the creative act that new possibilities and ideas are developed and brought forward out of the infinite depths of the consciousness that is God. These may then themselves become the foundations for new directions in creation. It is this understanding of creation that allows us as human beings to transform our higher inspiration and ideals into an eventual living reality. Only when we imagine and believe something to be possible, do we open the door to the Universe and draw the potential forward for it to become a reality.

The forefront of our present scientific theories and discoveries, as regards the nature and evolution of the Universe, is already touching upon these ideas, although most scientists are still restricted by their linear and mechanical views of creation. The standard theory of the big bang proposed that the entire Universe began its creation from one gigantic explosion, through which it expanded, cooled and formed the stars. At some point its expansion will cease (according to when its original explosive energy is used up) and it will begin to collapse back in upon itself. Since then inflationary theories have arisen, and more recently it was discovered, much to the amazement of many scientists who believed the expansion of the Universe would have to be slowing down, that the expansion of the Universe and separation of some galaxies had actually speeded up (not that any singular relative speed can be calculated for something that is continually opening and closing, and bringing new life into creation). This though has led to the acceptance of the fact that there is an invisible source of energy to the Universe that science had not discovered and could not measure. At this point the ability to measure and relate the Universe breaks down, and beyond this point our understanding of the Universe comes only through our conscious union and self-realisation. As science approaches the realisation of an infinite resource of energy to the Universe, which is continually bringing new creations into being and which is affected and directed by thought and consciousness, so all of its measurements become so ridiculously large or small that they become meaningless to our daily lives; in many scientific calculations infinity if still registered as an error. It is here that we begin to discover what God truly is, and why we are inseparable from this infinity.

Admittedly my knowledge of present scientific theory and terminology is in no way as vast or deep as some; I have not spent a vast number of years dedicated to its study, so I apologise if my ideas seem a little simplified or raw. I have however endeavoured to convey these concepts in a way that everybody can appreciate. I would challenge any present physicist, cosmologist or astronomer in the world today, to take the basic framework of this concept of solar formation and map it on to their own theories and discoveries, and then deny that it is possible. As to its complete authenticity: well it is just one way of expressing an idea, and I don't doubt there will be many more to come, which I shall look forward to. This is a Universe I know and experience through my heart and soul, in every moment of every day; it leaves no doubt in my mind, and has bred fulfilment and wholeness.

Planes Of Existence

As a solar system begins the process of its formation, different potential Planes of Existence are set up and established throughout the energy of the vortices. These planes exist on a conscious energy level rather than a physical level, and are accessible only through the mind on a level (frequency) of spiritual consciousness. They act as if to step down the infinite potential energy of pure undivided spirit into the physical vibration of an individual spiritual creation.

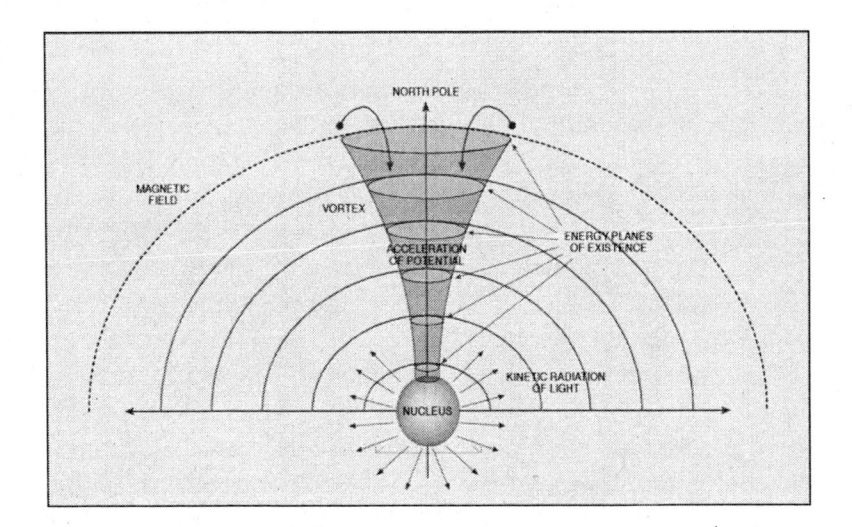

[Diagram: Cross-section showing NORTH POLE, MAGNETIC FIELD, VORTEX, ACCELERATION OF POTENTIAL, ENERGY PLANES OF EXISTENCE, KINETIC RADIATION OF LIGHT, NUCLEUS]

Each plane acts as a conscious energy blueprint for all that is later to become a physical creation (this is where the maxim 'as above, so below' originates from). They direct potential energy down to the next plane and eventually through the nucleus out into three-dimensional space as light energy and elemental building blocks. The original energy blueprint is carried within the light energy, which then begins to construct and evolve the desired physical creation (most commonly in the case of our solar system, a planet and all its forms of life) within the gaseous nebula of a newly forming star.

Each plane of existence is progressively worked down from its potential state, passed through the nucleus as the kinetic radiance of light, and established as evolving matter in a natural orbit around the Sun. The planets of our solar system are the physical reflections of the planes of existence within its vortices: they revolve in defined planes of orbit and radiate the conscious energy of the plane they represent. Every physical action and interaction is a direct reflection of the potential that is first formed within the planes of the vortices. It is from a direct conscious relationship with these planes that the ancient myths of the Gods first originated, which have since passed on their names to the physical planets that represent them.

Once all of the planes have been established in orbit as planetary bodies, then the channel of the vortices, between the inner solar system and the outer Universe, is completely open, and it can now draw in and guide individual spirits through the progressive physical incarnations of the entire solar system. In this way the original potential individual spirit gains its own real experience, knowledge and perspective of the Universe and the cycle of creation, from which it comes to form its own identity and spiritual entity: it becomes enlightened. The spirit describes the life force and the potential to become whole and aware, in communion with the source (God) and all other life. Whereas the soul is the individual entity, the degree to which the spirit has become enlightened and aware through incarnation and experience. In this respect the spirit is Universal through all things, binding us all to a singular state of origin, while the soul is completely unique, as no two beings occupy the same space at the same time and pass through the same individual experiences.

The Major Planetary Planes Of Our Solar System

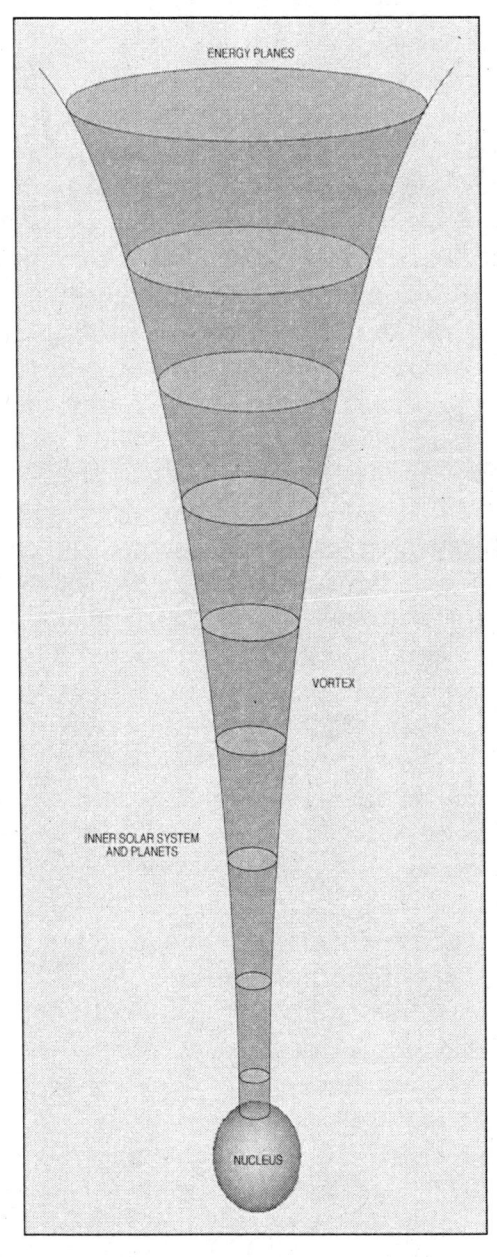

10th Plane: Pluto – the underlying energy directive behind all creation and destruction (life and death): the Universal will.

9th Plane: Neptune – the consciousness and feeling of Universal awareness: spiritual ideals and unconditional love.

8th Plane: Uranus – the conceptualisation of Universal awareness: the individual minds opening to love and spiritual ideals

7th Plane: Saturn – the physical limitations and potential of an individual within this creation: mastery of the elements

6th Plane: Jupiter – the impetus for an individual to explore and expand knowledge and experience: religious / cultural learning

5th Plane: Mars – individual will for the projection of spirit out into creation: self-assertion and vitality

4th Plane: Earth – conscious awareness of life and spirits relationship with individual nature: our personal mind

3rd Plane: Venus – sensual awareness of life and spirits relationship with individual nature: our personal feelings and senses

2nd Plane: Mercury – physical matter and concepts, and forms of communication: our bodily form and structures

1st Plane: Sun – the open hole and transformer through which all spirit comes into being: the nucleus and centre

There presently exists within our solar system, to the best of our knowledge, ten primary celestial bodies and levels of awareness: the Sun nucleus and nine planetary orbiting bodies. There are of course many other minor orbiting bodies and planetary moons, as well as comets, asteroids and meteoroids, all of which represent real interaction, but the major bodies are the ones we are all most aware of. These were all established and came into being as reflections of the original planes of existence within the vortices, the aim of which was to step down the infinite energy and consciousness of God into the temporal finite reality of our physical solar system. The planes that these bodies represent are not physical, they are levels of conscious energy that do not exist in time and space as we do; they are similar to our dream state, and upon them our consciousness is not restricted in its capacity to feel, visualise and imagine.

Everything that comes into a physical existence first originates as a directive of the Universal will, the intelligent source of the Universe, where it is formed as an energy blue print within the vortices and passed through the nucleus as light energy to manifest as a physical reality. A separate spiritual awareness that has the potential to develop its own entity of experience, is drawn like a droplet from the sea of potential to descend through the vortices, through the potential planes that will form the nature of its individual experience and awareness, and eventually manifests through the genetics of its chosen form within the temporal physical solar system.

This is how the Universe is in a completely open and interactive state, with new ideas and evolutionary directives being able to be introduced at any time: a solar system may open new doors and perspectives from the experience of its own evolution, and these can then be followed up within its own reality, and introduced and adapted to other star systems. Everything that exists in the physical Universe has reason, and is a reflection of the Universal will and its evolutionary directives. The emanations and orbits of the planets, other stars and galaxies, comets, meteoroids and asteroids, all reflect the energy interactions and directives from the higher levels of the vortices, and all have an affect upon and come to shape the individual natures of our spiritual being.

The individual spiritual entities (or souls) come to serve the Universal will that they are reflections of. They are the breath of life that breathes through the animal, vegetable and mineral kingdoms, and as they evolve and progress through these different states of being, so more spirit is drawn in and developed, ever continuing the cycle and progression. Those entities involved in the evolution of a particular solar system remain upon the planes of existence between incarnations, where they can assess the lessons and experiences they have passed through, and develop new ideas and prepare new experiences for the next incarnation. These planes represent energy levels as opposed to being defined within the co-ordinates of time and space; the planes are not physical as such but exist as consciousness, and souls are free to imagine and experience potential with little limitation. None of this experience becomes completely real and enlightened however, until the soul incarnates and transforms the potential, to experience it as a living reality, and in doing so the soul creates its entity and learns from direct experience of the cycle and nature of creation.

When a soul has completed its experience of the creative cycle and gained the complete self-awareness of its identity within God, it can freely move and incarnate outside of its own solar system. It has the knowledge of the complete experience of the Universe and an infinite potential of energy, imagination and intelligence at its disposal, and with this it may become the central opening and consciousness to a completely new star system. All of these potentials and ideas will be more easily related to as we delve into the evolution of our own human nature, for here we will find direct comparisons to our daily life and experiences.

Of course how we relate to and describe the idea of 'Universal will' may seem very different on the surface: what I call an evolutionary directive, a scientist may relate to as the nuclear reaction within the Sun that produces the elements and light radiation that precipitate life, while a priest may describe this as simply the will of God. They are all essentially the same thing, seen and expressed through different perspectives; none can genuinely claim to be any more righteous than the next, they are just different.

The Evolution Of Individual Spirits On Earth

As all the potential planes of existence slowly evolved and became established within our solar system, so a new channel for the evolution of individual spirits was opened upon the Earth. This was to create a direct link between the consciousness of the Earth and that of the Universe (God). This point marks the beginning of the separation in evolution between animals and humankind: there were already many individual conscious life forms evolving upon the Earth, and these had the potential to evolve further as mediums for the evolution of individual spiritual entities. The particular life form that became the focus for this further evolution of spirit was primitive man, ape-like and animal in its instincts.

The Seven Planes Of Man's Evolution

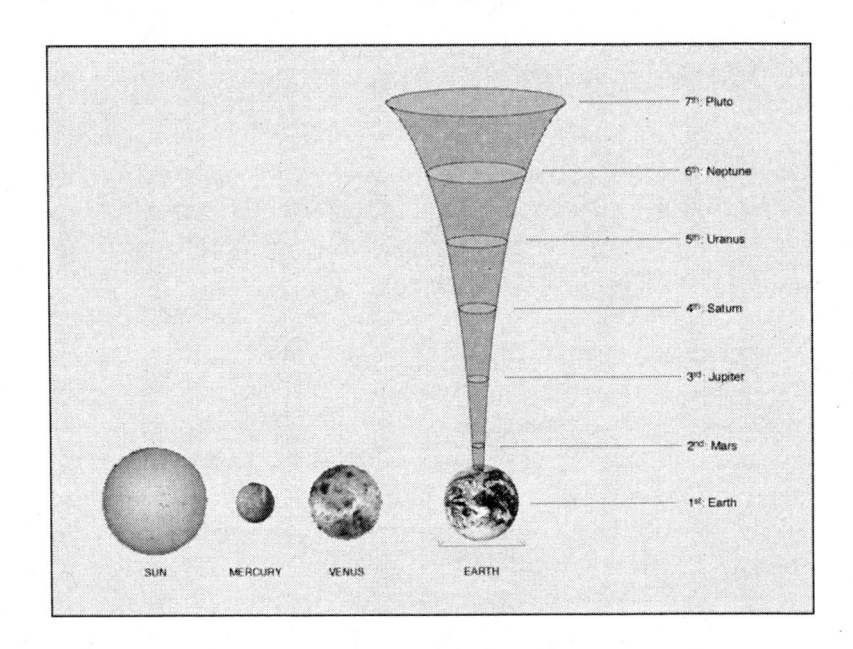

The light energy from the Sun that reaches the Earth, has passed through the Sun and between the orbits of Mercury, Venus and Earth, hence the nature and principles of these planes of existence are all fully established upon the Earth, and both individually and collectively as a race we are now evolving through the nature and principles of all the further planes of our solar system, from Mars to Pluto. Every man and woman alive is evolving through a vortex of potential planes, and when this is combined together as a collective reality, then each plane that mankind works through and transcends, is brought down to and established upon the Earth as our conscious living reality and level of awareness. Our human nature, that which is presently realised and our future potential, is composed of the combined nature of all the planes of existence within our solar system. By consciously evolving through the nature and awareness of these planes so we gain the experience (from our own unique perspective) of the full cycle of creation: we become unique spiritual entities. This then is a brief outline of the 7 primary planes of our human nature and evolution:

1ˢᵗ Plane: Earth:-

This first plane is the physical work base for all our unique experiences and evolution: the plane of incarnation. In this respect it is the main focus of our awareness and attention from which we draw a sense of stability, identity and reality. Without this grounded Earthly reality upon which we can individually move, experience and create, there would be no way of developing and enlightening our spiritual entity. The many souls that come here originate from the Universal will (they are created from God), and descend through the higher planes of existence, setting up the potential of their life experience. With each incarnation they gain more experience and more enlightenment, which comes to form their individual soul and awareness. The many souls that are incarnate at the present, seek different experiences and work from different levels of awareness, that combined together as our collective reality, forms the basic span of our morality and ethics, and these help to form the foundations of law within our societies: what is and is not commonly acceptable.

Upon this plane humankind develops a unique central identity, personality and radiant life force [representing the nature of the Sun]. We have a physical body and the dexterity that goes with it, which on a conscious level can be used to create solid concepts, words and forms of communication [Mercury]. We also have sensitivity and feeling to see, touch, hear, smell and taste our living environment, and to share this with others of our race [Venus]. And finally we have consciousness through which we can think, develop ideas, interact and explore our identity [Earth]. As the Earth is the planetary body associated with consciousness within our solar system, then much of our relationship with and learning of the higher planes of our existence comes through our individual conscious mind and its internal dialogue. From there it can be expressed and shared through the natures of the Sun, Mercury and Venus: through personality and self-expression, physical dexterity and concepts, and personal feelings and sensitivity. Each time we incarnate, our focus and awareness is first directed into developing the full nature of these planes through our infancy and childhood: we grow a body, we develop and explore our senses, we think and learn to utilise our minds. All of this comes to form our personality and radiant aura; it creates a centre and personal identity. After this is achieved and stabilised, so we pass through adolescence and into adulthood, and our awareness is drawn to return to continue evolving through the higher planes, according to our individual needs.

2nd Plane: Mars:-

The second plane is where we become more consciously aware of our own individual will and vitality of spirit, and where the nature of free will and personal ego are developed. The nature and impulse of Mars is to project strength and spirit forward out into the world, to develop the ability of self-assertion, increase our experience of life, and to take care of our most immediate needs for survival. From this plane we gain the knowledge that we are in control of how we direct ourselves upon the ground: the compulsion and impetus of what we need to experience to evolve comes from the destiny of our evolutionary directives, but we are free to interact with life and decide down which paths we project ourselves according to these directives.

Part of the learning experience of Mars may be the experience of anger, frustration and violence. Tension and pressure may build if we try to force our way down paths we have already experienced as opposed to moving forward in evolution and following new ones. This is an imbalance of desire that may expose what seems like a contradiction in human nature: we have free will, but it is subject to the directives of our higher spiritual nature and its needs to continue evolving, so in a sense we only have the illusion of free will, as it is the Universal will that ultimately dictates the direction of everything. It is a lesson that we can only learn from experience, and one that is clarified later as the impetus of the higher planes direct us to surrender or relinquish our personal will, so as to merge with and understand more the Universal will, and to experience a greater sense of communion.

3<u>rd</u> Plane: Jupiter:-

Upon this plane we are taught to direct our will and experience into all facets of life and human nature, to continually broaden our horizons and gain a greater knowledge of and relationship with all that the Earth and human nature has to offer. As our relationship with nature grows and expands and our understanding of its cycles and underlying spirit gets deeper, so the diversity of our many cultures have evolved: their rituals, philosophies and religions..., all of which are expressions of this growing relationship.

A sense of purpose and justice is bred through this plane, to direct our free will into furthering the knowledge and experience of humankind and providing for our collective needs, and it is from here that our human morality and social ideology originate, and so expand to encompass the wisdom (knowledge) of the higher planes. Individually we gain the impulse to crusade for our higher needs in evolution, which continues to liberate us from our more selfish animal instincts and expand our collective awareness and sense of responsibility. We learn that life is a two way flow: the more we give of ourselves, of our spirit, to step into the unknown and experience all that life has to offer, then the more inspiration and knowledge we gain in return, from the Universe, and the more we come to appreciate our true nature and identity as part of the Universe.

4th Plane: Saturn:-

Here is where we learn how to calm, pace and control our projection of will and purpose, to move with the tides of the Universe and master the lessons we have learnt. We are taught patience, durability and persistence over the experience of many life times, learning that there is much work to be done to bring our higher nature down to the Earth as a conscious living reality. It is on this plane that the very limits of our physical nature and experience are exposed, developing within us a greater strength and practical insight, although the restriction and responsibility of life can at times seem serious and heavy.

There is a strong element of teaching that we come to develop on this plane: as we begin to master the lessons of our own experience, so we become wiser to the ways of the world and those of human nature, and from this perspective we can stand firm to guide other souls on and upwards, along their own chosen paths of learning. Traditions and establishments stem from this plane, but we also must learn that to hold too stringently to tradition can lead to ignorance of the further potentials of our evolution that lie beyond, and from here stubbornness and dictatorial tendencies can build, that eventually lead to the destruction and disintegration of our establishments, thus allowing new thoughts and ideas to carry our evolution forwards again. All experiences and lessons, no matter how hard they may seem at the time, are a progression, and help to continue the expansion of our awareness.

5th Plane: Uranus:-

The impulse of Uranus can be summed up near enough in one word, 'eureka!' It breeds the inspiration to break through the traditional collective ways of thinking and develop our own individual intuitive link with the Universe. The dominance of our physical nature upon our perspective of life and personal identity, is gradually superseded by that of our spiritual. Uranus opens our consciousness to the eternity of spirit and the interconnectedness of the Universe, as well as enabling us to realise the independent and individual nature of our own entity.

Uranus is revolutionary and humanitarian: breaking open the structure and division of our cultures to expose the equality we may find in recognising our common spiritual source. We learn to use and respect our individual will as a unique medium for the expression of the Universal will, and in this way we come to serve the further expansion of the Universe's self-awareness and experience. Communication and knowledge of the Universe can now come to us through the open window of our mind, as a flow of higher intuition that gives us a direct relationship with God, the Universal mind. This unique connection to God can then find expression through our temporal personality and its individual human nature.

6*th* *Plane: Neptune:-*

Neptune works in a very subtle and yet overwhelming way, developing our highly sensitive spiritual nature and awareness. It is all embracing, dissolving the layers between our higher and lower states of mind and awareness. This enables us to feel and be completely immersed in the immense power and spirit of the Universe; that we are connected to and sensitive to all life. It is as if our mind may drift in the infinite ocean of potential that is God, experiencing the expanses of its imagination and spiritual ideals, which can then be channelled into the Earth and used to heal the imbalances in existing life and to raise its level of awareness, as well as being used for creating new life. Yet without proper grounding Neptune can lead to the experience of delusions, escapism and impractical dreaming, where a persons mind is distanced from its day-to-day reality.

So the balance between idealism and practice is important, if human nature is to be both imaginative and productive. We learn the nature of unconditional love through Neptune as our heart and central being is opened up completely, just as the nucleus of a star system is opened, and with this comparison you can appreciate the energy that is then available to us. This allows the Universe to live and breathe freely through us; we come to exist in a more selfless state of being that is moved and directed by the Universe and the needs of the life around us. Intuition, visualisation, clairvoyance and telepathy are all abilities of human nature that can be developed on this level; they are natural senses that extend beyond our ordinary physical senses, representing a more conscious interaction with energy and our evolutionary directives.

7*th* *Plane: Pluto:-*

This level leads us in to the unfathomable depths and root core of the infinite power and energy of creation, from which all life and Universal directives originate. This is where the Universal will begins the process of creation and manifestation, and on this level we complete our own evolutionary cycles to consciously merge with the creative will and power of the Universe. We become channels for the regenerative and transformative energies of creation, and can draw upon this energy to manipulate and manifest new creations, according to need and attraction and the Universal will (positive energy flows to a negative balance, and negative is drawn to a positive). In a sense we are turned completely inside out, where the conscious existence of our soul becomes eternal and this becomes our natural perception and state of being, thus dissolving the barriers between life and death. Here our spiritual entity, which is now wholly enlightened and a complete reflection of God, can choose to manifest or de-manifest at will, according to what the Universe requires. Our entity becomes a representative of the Universal will, an ambassador of God, and with the full experience of the complete cycle of a star system, we may now become the central opening and intelligence through which a new cycle and star system can begin.

The Nature Of Orbiting Moons

Many of the planets in our solar system have moons rotating in a fixed orbit about them, and as all bodies come to manifest and stabilise from an energy level and are the physical representations of the directives and interactions on these levels, so these moons have a purpose and meaning in our nature and evolution. In the main they represent different principles and areas of learning, intermediate levels, upon the plane of the planet they orbit, and in the case of the Earth, which has one orbiting moon, this represents a very distinct part of our own human nature: the subconscious medium of the mind and its instinctive emotional responses.

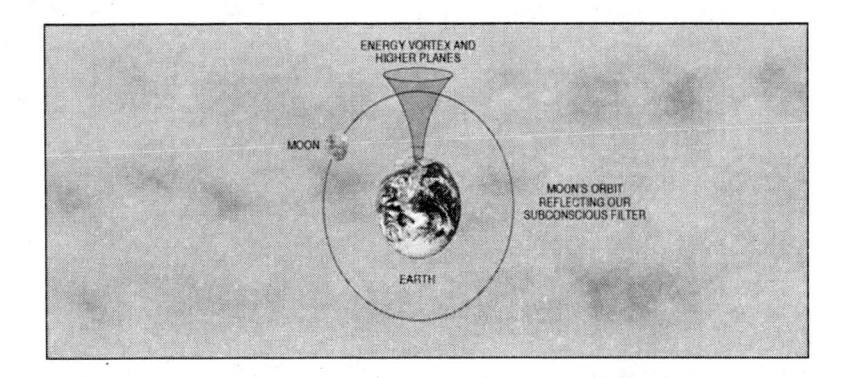

[Diagram: Earth with Moon in orbit. Labels: ENERGY VORTEX AND HIGHER PLANES; MOON; MOON'S ORBIT REFLECTING OUR SUBCONSCIOUS FILTER; EARTH]

Every time a soul incarnates upon the Earth as a human being, in its early and emotionally supple formative years, as a baby and later as a child, it develops a unique sensitive bond to life. This is an emotional nature that is the construct of both its evolved level of spiritual awareness (carried in the soul from past experience), and more directly, of its early treatment and experience; according to the atmospheres, environments and people it is surrounded by. Babies are much more sensitive and aware than we may yet appreciate, but as they have not yet developed the abilities to communicate in the human ways we most readily look for and recognise, it is difficult to understand how their early experiences affect the nature of the personality they grow to be. Babies are very open and sensitive beings; they are souls reacquainting themselves with human form, with few resistances or blocks to their supple nature. Many of our instinctive reactions and emotional responses to people and situations in later life, have their foundations in the nature of our earliest experiences.

These early experiences come to build a subconscious medium within the delicate fabric of our mind. It is a type of veil between the conscious awareness of our present personality and lifetime, and the conscious experience of many previous lifetimes that go to make up our enlightened spiritual entity. The nature of this subconscious medium, that both protects and helps to focus our present Earthly consciousness, and acts as a filter through which the knowledge and inspiration of the higher mind can descend, is physically represented within our solar system by the Moon and its orbit around the Earth. In the same way that the Moon carves a sheltering orbit that encompasses the Earth, so its subconscious veil surrounds and protects our present Earthly consciousness.

If our subconscious responses to life remain optimistic, open and well balanced, then the filter remains clear and easily accessible, and as we pass through adolescence and grow older, we may draw upon the knowledge and experiences of previous lives (that can find ways to manifest in the present), and tap the inspiration and guidance of our needs to grow and learn in the present. The foundations set in early life are never so solid that they cannot change, adapt and transform throughout life, if they could not then our personality would consolidate, stagnate and eventually disintegrate. But, if a person were to become weighed down by early traumatic experiences and the confused emotions that accompanied them (indeed even a traumatic experience in later life), then the subconscious divide may become dark and dense, confused by unresolved anger or fear, and this may act as a block to the knowledge and support of the higher mind. The fear, confusion and frustration trapped by the subconscious naturally seeks release, and if we do not allow this naturally and attempt to rebuild the subconscious fabric, then perversions and complexities of our nature and personality can develop. These then begin to destroy our connection to soul and the higher mind, and distort and manipulate our conscious perspective of life. The natural positive flow of spirit and higher consciousness can be twisted and turned as it passes through the confused subconscious, and by the time it is expressed upon the ground, it can seem negative and destructive. This is the root cause of most mental illnesses, disorders and stresses, all of which will eventually find balance and understanding as part of the progression of life; even the unresolved emotions of previous lives find ways to manifest in future ones so that they can be resolved and we can learn from the experience and continue to progress.

We each develop a new framework of subconscious responses and expressions with every life that we come to live, and these combined together for all humanity represent our collective subconscious: the totality of our personal thoughts, actions, fears and emotions. The collective subconscious is more commonly referred to as the astral plane, linked to the Akashic records: it is the living interacting energy imprint of all human personalities and experience, and of all the presently unresolved emotions [karma] of the human race that seek resolution and release. Individually our conscious awareness of life and the nature of our actions works with and affects our collective reality as a race: the more people that live with a positive mental attitude and co-operative spirit, to remain open and balanced, then the more this way of life is supported for the whole human race. So as we choose to accept more individual responsibility for our life and our actions, so we come to affect and support the collective evolution of the whole human race. We may seem like one grain of sand in over six and a half billion, but we all have our part to play and leave our reflections and imprints upon the collective.

An immense amount of our time on Earth is spent in a sleeping state. Not only do we physically rest and regenerate our bodies during sleep, but also our minds and subconscious. During sleep our mental focus is drawn to the astral plane where we have the freedom and ability to work upon and absorb past experience, assess our present, and even prepare for possible future events. Dreams represent very real experiences and visualisations upon the astral plane. They can evoke powerful emotions and symbolism's, that can be a way for our subconscious to make us more aware of certain things we may be neglecting in full waking consciousness (which is one of the reasons why some of the symbolism can be very obscure and strange at times). When translating and understanding dreams it is essential to look at the feelings they evoke rather than the visualisations our minds have attached to these, for this is where the real work of the subconscious and its energy interactions are revealed. At present we live almost a third of our lives upon this astral plane: our consciousness can draw experience from the past..., interact with other souls..., work upon its own subconscious..., visualise the potential future..., or just explore the vast realms of collective human experience. While not physical in the way we appreciate day-to-day life, it is a real place that offers real experience.

Each of our individual subconscious veils and natures also helps to protect us from the mass of interactions and 'noise' of the collective subconscious. If the subconscious fabric of a persons mind is damaged by some traumatic experience, or by the feeding of negative self-destructive emotions, then the confusion and interactions of the collective subconscious (the unresolved emotions and karma of others) can also be drawn in to interfere with the mind and consciousness of a person, which again is a cause of many of our delusions and mental illnesses.

While the root cause and development of every perversion and complexity of human nature is personal to the individual, and should be treated as such to retrace and resolve the problem, there are two main reasons why mental illness develops and the subconscious becomes damaged or blocked. Both reasons stem from a relinquishing of responsibility towards our life and actions, and until this is taken back in hand and a willingness to resolve the problem is employed, then healing cannot take place and the problem cannot be fully resolved.

The first reason is mainly due to a withdrawal of spirit and willingness to live life, because of a lack of desire to face up to and work through the harder more difficult, traumatic experiences. This weak resolve opens the subconscious up to damaging influences according to the fear or difficult experiences that caused it. The void left by the withdrawal of spirit can draw in and be filled with a reflection of the persons fear, and the disruptive influences (even 'voices' in some cases) within the collective subconscious. The second reason is mainly due to a person's wilful resistance to facing their unresolved feelings and heeding their conscience. In this case the problem may again stem from difficult experiences or inflated desires, but whatever the reason, their natural behaviour becomes manipulated and distorted. Due to this wilful resistance to heed what is after all our own natural reaction, and a conscious decision to feed these destructive emotions, then negative feelings and emotions, which are essentially self-destructive, can build within a person and force their way out in more damaging ways. This cycle of building and releasing will continue until the problem is retraced, faced and resolved. Again the subconscious can become damaged and blocked, denying the person the feeling and inspiration of the higher mind to progress in life, and leaving them facing the growing obsession and problem until the subconscious is once more cleared. In some cases it is not faced until we pass out of life, and so has to be resolved in a future incarnation.

I have not gone into great depth here as I am only trying to outline the basic self-regulating nature of the subconscious and human psyche, which in essence is the nature and origin of the idea of karma. All our experiences and emotions have something to offer and teach us, but if we do not face and work through the harder more confrontational experiences of life, then the naturally open and free expression of our evolving nature and awareness can become blocked and distorted. All illness has the potential to be healed and will eventually find resolution, even if it takes many lifetimes of experience to break the cycle and learn our lessons. Of course if the root of a problem lies in a previous life then it is much more difficult to consciously trace and to understand why it has manifested in our present life, but there are always reasons and causes, and behind these lies the understanding and lessons we need to evolve, to realise our true nature and identity within the Universe.

If we take a psychological illness that involves damage to the subconscious, say under the wide term of schizophrenia as an example, and then treat this medically as something physiological or neurological because we do not understand the nature of the illness, and so use drugs to affect the brain's natural state. Then we may subdue a person's illness but we will never help to resolve it or heal it in this manner. I have heard of doctors and psychologists telling people that there is no cure for such mental illnesses, when all this reflects is their own lack of understanding as to the nature of the problem and their lack of openness to search for answers.

Admittedly the nature of a person's psychological illness and all that has developed from it, can in some cases become very complex. But while it may take much time and hard work, there is always a way back to the root and the potential to uproot and heal the problem, no matter how deep. The first step and priority to healing is a person's willingness to be healed and their commitment to face the problem. From here a psychologist can help, guide and support the process if they are needed, but they cannot actually do the work for a person. The person themselves has to break down the patterns that have developed, retrace the problem to its roots, release it, and go on to repair the fabric of the subconscious. It could be the work of a lifetime, or indeed of many lifetimes. For a psychologist to understand and support the healing of a deep psychological illness, they themselves must have a personal depth of experience in their own psychology and subconscious, to be able to enter into the mind of another and accompany their journey. True psychological understanding cannot be learnt from a book, as with all knowledge, it requires personal experience to learn, understand and appreciate.

These then are the primary planes and levels of awareness that combined together go to make up our human nature; that which we have realised and that which is our future potential. The evolutionary imperative of our soul and spirit as it enters into human nature, is to embrace life, to progress, learn and evolve. Individually and collectively we are driven by the impulses of each plane to explore and develop that part of our nature, until eventually our focus and awareness transcends to the next plane, and with each level that is integrated into our nature, so we become more enlightened as to our purpose and identity within the Universe. The planes are not separate in the sense that we can only work upon one at a time; all our experiences in life (whether we are conscious of it or not) are helping to develop and integrate the potentials of all the planes.

The incarnate souls of our present day exist and work on many different levels of awareness: some are learning, some teaching, some creating, some destroying and some healing, and whether we are aware of it or not, we are all working together as a race to expand our awareness and achieve a greater sense of communion. We all have soul and are equal in our potential, it is down to our strength of will and sense of purpose how we evolve and through which experiences: to continue to walk forward and shed light on the unknown is the only way we can truly grow.

The Natural Cycle Of Reincarnation

In the present day reincarnation is still a topic of debate and opinion, a matter of personal belief that we may choose to believe in or not according to what suits our frame of mind and our personal perspective of life. Yet this is just our way of getting used to the concept: in the past most people had no comprehension of the idea..., today nearly everyone is aware of the idea of reincarnation and has an opinion on it..., and tomorrow it will be an ordinary and naturally accepted part of our existence. To our soul it is a natural cycle, and regardless of what we choose to believe at present, it is a reality for all of us, for the energy of soul never dies. Of course we will all have to find this out in our own time and in our own way.

When our body, our Earthly base and physical connection to life, can no longer sustain itself, either through weariness or due to the fact that our needs and lessons for this particular life have been fulfilled and there is no more we can achieve, then the life force and awareness is withdrawn from the Earthly plane and its temporal personality. Now it can absorb and share the lessons and ideas of its recent experience and prepare the way for the next incarnation (if necessary). This is the experience of death that many of us still face and look upon with much trepidation and fear, simply because our selfish animal instinct for survival still dominates our perspective and denies our whole hearted acceptance of this inevitable passing. Yet without this fear of death we would be able to explore the experience and enter into it in more depth, gaining a greater understanding of the nature of this transition. It is clear to see the still primitive nature of our modern societies that pour so much time and resources into the desperate search for longevity and some sort of power over death, when the only power over death and sight beyond, comes from our acceptance of it. The only power that death has over us is the fear that we continue to project upon it in our reluctance to face its inevitability, for while we continue to draw our identity from our physical being and personality, then we will always fear its loss and passing, and fail to see what lives beyond.

The first thing we confront after death and must release ourselves from, having passed from a more physical state of being and awareness back to a spiritual one, is the individual nature and subconscious patterns of the personality and ego we had grown to identify ourselves with. This is the covering veil between the conscious Earthly experience of one lifetime and the enlightened spiritual entity of many lifetimes experience, and as we release ourselves from the physical bonds of the personal ties, relationships and emotions that we had formed with the time, people and places of our lifetime's experience, so our Earthly consciousness merges with the spiritual whole and our lessons and experiences become fully absorbed and established within our soul.

If in passing through death we are unable to let go of all of our ties, due to the fact we carried over many fears and unresolved emotions [negative karma] from that lifetime, then when we come to reincarnate again, this confusion can be carried over in our reconnection to the next life. Again this a natural reflection of what we need to experience, helping us to face what is unresolved so that we might continue to learn and progress; the challenge of life may seem much harder in this respect, but the joy of overcoming will always feel much greater, and the lessons we learn will be that much more certified.

Once we have left the body and physical plane we no longer have the physical senses (sight, hearing, touch, taste and smell) to relate to things. We exist as an energy state, as a spiritual entity, and as such we relate to things in their pure energy state, embracing, entering into and feeling the essence of the whole. To understand near death experiences and out of body experiences, we then need to appreciate the nature of this spiritual sensitivity: while outside the body our existence is much more fluid and interconnected, our awareness can move its focus of attention and pass through matter, to sense and experience things beyond the scope of the body. But when we return to the body and come to translate these experiences in an energy state, we are then limited by the images and visualisations of our personal mind: hence the nature of these experiences can be very similar, and yet our descriptions of them may differ greatly (the people we meet, the places we go to, etc..).

Once we are released from the personal ties of what is now a previous life, then the awareness of our spiritual entity may return to the higher planes of our existence, to share itself and merge with other entities, and to support and guide those still upon the Earth. The feelings that those still alive hold for us in their hearts, act as a line and doorway through which we can support and guide them from the higher planes. In a sense we continue to share and grow with them, only the communication is spiritual and so subtle that few as yet are directly conscious of it. Most people tend to look for communication through their physical senses and hold on to the physical images of those that have passed on, mourning the loss of what they had become accustomed to. It is this sadly that tends to block the spiritual communication that continues after death. Still, as our awareness and understanding of death grows, so will our fear of it disintegrate and our spiritual sensitivity increase: we will eventually come to celebrate the passing of a life as we rejoice in the birth of one, and continue to share with it beyond the present divide of death.

Upon the higher planes of our existence all things exist as a pure state of energy. The potential for visualisation and imagination, and for developing new ideas for future incarnations is virtually unlimited, compared to the present limits of our physical confinement on Earth. Upon every plane lies the knowledge of the collective experience of all human beings that relates to that particular plane, and these energy imprints act as libraries that we may draw knowledge from and learn from in preparation for our future incarnations. These libraries in a sense are the books of life, containing the feelings and experiences of all previous incarnations and personalities, and upon these planes we can enter into and pass through these experiences to help expand our own awareness and perspective. In a way these books of life are now reflected in our present physical world, exposed by the increasing number of biographies available on our bookshelves that allow us to walk through others lives and thoughts. Of course not all of these will tell the whole story as is imprinted within the energy planes, and many are coloured with personal desire and interpretation. Nevertheless they seem to capture our interest and curiosity and help to expand our awareness.

When an entity decides to reincarnate and enter into human form once more, then the time, place, environment and physical genetics are all chosen according to its needs to evolve in that lifetime. All the conditions are freely chosen by the soul that is to incarnate to help its continued evolution, even those of physical and mental disability. A person that is born without sight or limbs, or without the ability to directly speak and communicate, is forced to adapt, and their focus is drawn to other areas of their nature where an immense amount can be achieved; such a life offers great challenge and great potential for learning. For those working with and living with the disabled, they too have to meet the challenge and are forced to look at themselves in more depth. Needing to be cared for and caring for someone who is disabled, can help immensely to open us up and to generate great amounts of love. Collectively this teaches us responsibility for all human beings, no matter what their physical or mental state may be, for we are all born with the same human rights. Conditions of disability, whether through birth or ones sustained later in life, are always freely chosen by the souls involved, our experiences are never forced upon us (even if we may not consciously appreciate them) and they always have a positive purpose; if we are not listening to our soul, then we may not always agree with what it delivers unto us.

As all life is interconnected and interactive, so every incarnation is a reflection of the evolved nature and awareness of the Universe as a whole. The basic positions and interrelationships of the planets at the time and place of birth, in alignment with the radiant energies of the constellations, all represent the expressive nature and underlying energies to be drawn in and worked through in any particular incarnation: the strengths of planes to be shared and the potential to be brought forward and developed. Astrology, when used with an open mind and understood correctly, is one way of mapping the potential energies and their characteristic human expressions, which are made available to a soul at birth. No two souls are born in exactly the same place at exactly the same time, and the major factor as to how a soul makes use of the Universal energy it is born as a reflection of, is the unique evolved nature of the individual soul itself. In this respect we are all different, and we all react to similar situations and circumstances in different ways. A birth chart is only a general representation of an individual's present energy and nature, the person themselves is the living reality and should always remain the central focus for their decisions in life.

Where Astrology can be very useful is in helping us to look deeper within ourselves: it can help us to recognise some of our habits, responses and patterns in life, where our weaknesses and strengths lie, and why we experience some of the things we do in life. It is also a very useful tool for diagnosis, for tracing problems and blockages back to their roots. Ultimately Astrology offers a more Universal perspective to life that may put us more in touch with ourselves and our needs to evolve. It is a guide we can use to support our own feelings and instincts, and should never be valued above these. Those who use it for prediction or as the determining factor in their decision making process, often carry it beyond its most useful means.

All spiritual movement of preparation and rebirth is as one continuous natural flow, directed by the Universal will and in harmony with the needs of the evolving human race. A life plan is not a fixed mental script to be acted out, as it is continually open and interactive, with new ideas and directions able to be introduced by our higher mind at any time, according to how our experience is going. A life plan represents the original potential for our higher mind to evolve, it is an intuitive flow to our Earthly consciousness and personality, guided by our spiritual entity and ultimately by the Universal will [God], and we are fed just enough understanding and motivation to keep us striving along the correct Earthly paths of experience. This is how to bring out the greatest amount of potential, for if we knew all the answers and directions beforehand there would be little challenge in life and very little work done in achieving our aims. It is this constant adaptability and interaction that helps to develop new ideas and directions in creation, and without it we would develop very little self-identity as spiritual entities.

When a spiritual entity incarnates, it enters into the physical genetics of whatever life form it is to grow into and experience. These physical genetics are a seed, much like a plant seed, that contain the information and structure of the complete evolution and present nature of that particular life form (in our case the nature of a human being). The genetics continue to evolve and adapt with each new generation of experience, and, if it is so desired to expand awareness and create new ideas, then any spiritual entity, that may of developed and evolved in another star system, can enter into and experience the genetics of any other being in any other star system, provided its consciousness is prepared and developed enough. In this way what we might consider to be an alien entity can actually enter into and evolve as a human being, if they needed to experience that perspective of the Universe, or to help the evolution of our consciousness as a race. Consciously we would know no different, as they would be as human as anyone else, and in this respect there is no such thing as an alien entity, as all beings are part of the same evolving Universe and family.

I don't doubt that there are other evolved life forms and spiritual entities that have and still do guide or own evolution on Earth. As we would experiment with the genetics of animals, so they in the same respect may experiment with human genetics (although in a much more responsible and advanced manner than we do at present). It is in no way malevolent, as the Universe and all its evolved life forms work in communion and co-operation. It is just the Universe making practical use of its available resources. Our present fear and paranoia as regards alien invasion, only exposes the still primitive nature of our awareness and understanding, which in time will be worked out of our system as consciousness evolves. Indeed in the present day much of our fascination with aliens and UFOs works to uproot and exorcise our fears, as a preparation for and introduction to the reality of other intelligent life forms. Until we can overcome this primitive fear however, then for obvious reasons we will not be ready to communicate with and interact with other life forms on a global scale.

The genetics of a human being is produced by the combination of male and female counterparts, and the sexual act that brings these two together is presently another area of confusion in our transition from animal to spiritual nature and awareness. Our sexuality works and exists on two different levels: on the level of our animal nature the sexual act is a selfish, competitive and sometimes violent instinct, driven by the compulsion to reproduce and survive as a species. Whereas on a spiritual level, sex is transformed to an act of love and affection, where two souls open themselves up and merge with each other. Again as we pass through the transition we are torn between the two, and our obsession with sex as a race, I believe, comes from the fact that it can be one of the most natural, passionate, emotive and creative experiences of our entire lives.

There has never been any sin in sex itself, for it is our personal motivations that speak of our reasoning and thus affects our karma Spiritually, sex is a natural and free act to be shared, explored and enjoyed between freely consenting beings. As soon as there is pressure, manipulation or force, then it becomes an act against human rights. Sadly the falsified shame, repression and fear we have at times been fed about sex and sexuality (often through religious dogma), has only served to force sexual expression and energy into the recesses of our private minds, which in turn can lead to the repressed outbursts and abuse that have become so prevalent in our present societies around the world. Sexuality is a beautiful and creative energy we all naturally posses.

Confusion, however, does now exist between our genetic compulsion to reproduce and our need to share love and intimacy. As we continue to open up spiritually and become more sensitive to each other, so the gender roles of male and female become less defined, and our need to share affection has merged with our sexual instincts and desires. Rape and sexual abuse expose the more destructive elements of the confusion in our sexuality, as the repressed need to express and share love and affection is distorted by the desire to have sex and take this from another. The painful experiences of this confusion are in the long run helping us to evolve, so that eventually we might come to experience the pleasures and depths of love and affection more in our everyday lives. Our spiritual sensitivity and bonding is increasing, and sex is no longer the only medium through which we can express this joy. Of course sex will continue between those who freely consent and are drawn to each other, with our genetic reproduction continuing as long as the experience of the human race is needed by the Universe. But the more damaging realities of rape and abuse will die out, as we learn to express our sexuality and love for each other in more open and complete ways.

Obviously not everyone in our present day is directly aware of these realities and the nature of reincarnation, but there are some, and the ideas are gradually evolving into our consciousness so that they may soon become established as our natural understanding and awareness. When we reach this level of understanding there is very little room, if any, for the destructive tendencies of hatred, war and violence. It may sound idealistic in the light of our present societies, but it is undeniably our potential as a race. For the moment as we receive the majority of our impulses and inspiration to go forward in life, through the filter of our subconscious, all we can do is trust to follow the instincts that are most natural to us and pray that these will lead us where we need to go. We each have to find our own answers and fulfil our own doubts, so that we may come to be certain of the truths to our existence. Again my thoughts and ideas are put forward in a general way, and I'm sure there are many people who would choose to express these ideas in a different way. Hopefully though these thoughts and ideas may help to open the doorway to a new perspective on life, one in which you are free to step through to fill in the details....

The Self-Regulating Nature Of Karma

All forms of creation, from atoms to planets to stars, are composed of a structured balance of kinetic energy expanded about a central core, within a specific amount of three-dimensional space. The core is an opening for energy to pass through to enable growth and expansion: it is the medium through which all elements and light energy are produced in a star, just as it is the medium for the large amounts of energy that can be released when the structure of an atom is altered or broken down. For the structure and evolution of an atom, planet or star to remain stable and consistent, there is a need to maintain a balance of energy: the outward projective force of energy for a physical structure and form of life, thus experiences an equal negative inward force, to maintain the stability and balance of the structure. At it simplest level this is a natural self-regulating balance between the positive expansion of kinetic light energy and the negative implosion of the void of space. Without this balance nothing would remain manifest, as it would either implode in upon itself or explode outwards. The self-regulating nature of this balance means that it is completely interactive and adaptable, according to the evolutionary expansion of whatever form and being is evolving and growing. In this way it holds the structure of a form together, but allows it to evolve and increase or decrease in energy and matter (as with the recently discovered increase in the rate of the Universe's expansion, relative to the acceleration of galaxies).

From a scientific viewpoint what we are essentially looking at is the force of gravitation: the property of mutual attraction possessed by all bodies of matter. This exposes the totally interconnected nature of the Universe, with all bodies acting on each other, no matter how large or small. Most scientists tend to look at this force from the perspective of its inward force and acceleration towards the centre or core of something, and yet from the other side it exposes the outward generative radiation of life [energy] from something, which I feel offers a more positive perspective to understanding gravitation and how all life forms interact with and effect each other.

Gravitation is the perfectly poised balancing force that holds everything in its place within creation and exposes the interconnected relationship of all bodies and matter. One body falling out of the balance of its orbit, thus has a knock-on effect to all other bodies. For the Universe to remain stable in its structure and to continue evolving and projecting more energy and matter into being, then it needs a self-regulating force that can adapt and react, and this is the true nature and purpose of gravitation and the balance it maintains: the outward radiant energy force for every being and type of matter, experiences and equal inward force (that of the negative implosion of space). It is this inward force that science presently refers to as the force of attraction between bodies of matter.

Now we only need to expand this idea of gravitation slightly to appreciate the self-regulating nature of karma, which is essentially the same thing. Newton's third law of motion (which in itself is a Universal law of creation) states that, to every action or expression of energy there is an equal and opposite reaction. When we expand this law into all aspects of human nature (our thoughts, feelings and actions) then we have defined the self-regulating nature of karma. Karma is in no way the act of retribution or the punishment we are given for being bad in the eyes of God, it is quite simply the natural law that maintains our stability and growth as evolving spiritual entities.

If we view our evolutionary projection as a momentum that directs our expanding consciousness upwards through the experiences of the many planes of our human nature, then any active learning experience that destabilises this momentum and throws our direction off at a tangent, will, in the goodness of time, experience a reaction that brings our evolutionary momentum back into line. Far from being a judgement as to right and wrong, our conscience represents our own personal development of awareness through the experience of karma, teaching us of the nature and direction of our evolution and the governing laws of the Universe. In this respect our personal experience of karma is an all-important factor as to our learning of lessons and conscious enlightenment. It is no good to dictate what is right or wrong to another, for the simple reason that we each must develop our own conscience from experience to truly expand our consciousness and awareness, it is an evolutionary directive of our nature. Of course the level of conscience that we adhere to and live by naturally, comes to affect the collective, and in doing so it supports and strengthens the development of the whole human race. In essence this is where our responsibility lies, with our own actions and karma, and as we focus upon and work and grow through this, so we can help to break down the destructive patterns [greed, violence, abuse] that still exist within our collective human nature.

Through the painful emotional experiences of fear, confusion, anger, violence and abuse, so we come to appreciate the transition between the two levels of our nature (the selfish lower animal nature and the selfless higher spiritual nature), and the nature of our conscience is gradually formed and developed. Our wilfully destructive actions do not so much reflect in what we impose upon others, although their reaction to this can affect their own karma and learning, it reflects back on ourselves and what we need to learn to progress in life. Karma has many ways to restore and maintain balance in our nature and its evolutionary momentum, it is not a cold mechanical reaction that physically recreates every action we have projected, so that we experience exactly the same things that we do to others. Karma works more on an energy level and can be worked out co-operatively between souls.

If we do perpetrate an ignorant act that hurts or offends someone and creates a dilemma within our own conscience (which may for a while halt our evolutionary momentum), then the reaction to this is an equal and opposite energy reaction to the original act that was perpetrated. As we acknowledge this reaction and work back through the experience to appreciate the more balanced approach, so we learn its wisdom, develop our conscience, and evolve in our human nature and understanding. How this reaction of energy manifests itself and gets us to acknowledge and accept it can be brought about in many different ways, according to the experiences we choose and what we need to learn. Some may soul search and freely acknowledge their conscience, to work through and clear the negative imprint of an action. Others may be put through an experience that forces them to acknowledge responsibility for what they have done and learn from it. While some may even have to go through the traumatic experience of what they themselves have put upon another, before they can appreciate what they have done and accept to resolve their own actions.

If we view a soul evolving in isolation, then there is little resistance to its momentum and it can simply realise its potential. But this creates few challenges and gives little room for developing individual character. Now if we bring together billions of souls within the scope of the same nature and environment, then their web of interactions and reactions, helps to stimulate their unique evolution and develop support and communion between souls (that reflects the interconnected nature and spirit of the Universe). This is what helps to create uniquely individual entities, and it is the self-regulating nature of karma that gives stability to this collective form of evolution

Karma works in many ways, and although we are not always conscious of the fact, it is our decision as to the paths of learning we take. Ultimately we need to learn to forgive ourselves (as forgiveness represents the acknowledgement and release of karma), in the same way that we need to learn to forgive others. Forgiveness is of course not just a dismissal of our actions, as it requires an acceptance of responsibility and a release of unresolved emotions. All experience, once we allow it to, will lead to a greater understanding of life, as long as we are willing to dig deep enough to appreciate the whys of our conscience. Until we are willing, then the patterns of our destructive actions will remain with us, and although it is common sense and has been said many times before: to react to violence with more violence, will only increase the violence, ill feeling and confusion, and create more karma and problems for us to work through. In the short term, it can at times seem frustrating that some people act as if without conscience and give the false impression that they can get away with their actions. But no perpetrator of an injustice or destructive action can ever escape having to face up to its repercussions and to taking responsibility. Our actions and their reactions define our very nature and remain with us always as the imprints and pathways that have led us to our present enlightenment.

Karma does of course work in a positive manner: what we give of ourselves emotionally and creatively throughout life, to the people, time and place we live in, we will in time receive back in our joy and appreciation of living and the positive enlightenment and strength of our soul. The gravity of karma is natural and simple, we need not become over concerned with it as it is completely self-regulating and works according to need and attraction: whatever we need in life to experience and learn (relationships, resources, knowledge), either it is attracted to us or we are compelled and energised to seek it out...; we need only to trust our heart felt instincts and intuition. While essentially our karma works on an individual level according to our actions, it does also have to be resolved in more collective ways, as regards families, local communities, nations and the actions and experiences of the human race as a whole. Wherever there is a form of identity then karma is at work, maintaining growth and stability.

Our understanding of karma and our responsibilities lie not so much in what we are told to think, but as with all things, in our own human instincts and the nature and voice of our conscience. There is no destructive action, that we have put upon ourselves or upon the nature of the Earth, that will not in time experience a reaction and have to be faced up to. This fact in itself should compel us to look more honestly at the ways of the world we have created around us and to take a greater responsibility for our part in it. Mass economics and industrialisation are very small minded and immature foundations for society, that wantonly abuse the Earth's natural resources and destabilise its natural cycles. Again it is just a case of how far down this path we choose to go and how much we need to experience as a reaction, before we learn our lessons and move beyond.

As all life originates from an infinite source of motionless conscious potential energy, then anything that is actively drawn out of this to form a star system and all the life contained within, eventually experiences a reaction and returns to its original balanced state, leaving only the conscious entities developed by the experience. The white hole of a star system opens, manifests and evolves a creative reality and experience, gradually breaks down and disintegrates passing on its energy, and collapses in upon itself as the black hole closes. As regards our own planet, its structure is held together and maintains a stable orbit around the Sun as an integral part of the solar system, with its own gravity keeping our feet on the ground and enabling us to experience the wonders of this existence on Earth. All nature is self-regulating, maintaining a consistent evolutionary momentum of growth, while regulating the balance of its natural cycles and ecosystems. So it is with human nature, with our conscious evolution being self-regulated by conscience and karma, and as our souls gradually become more enlightened as to their true Universal identity, so we overcome gravitation, and are set free of the cycle of karma to explore the entire Universe.

Love, Light and Healing

As human beings we have no choice but to love; it is a part of our nature that we shall all eventually come to live by.

Love

Rather than being just the emotional feelings we experience from close relationships, I have come to understand and experience love as an actual state of being that is part of our naturally evolving human nature. Granted at present most of our learning experiences of love come from our experiences of personal relationships. But many of these relationships also involve the exposure of our fears and dependencies, which rather than being part of the nature of love, is something that love tends to expose in our vulnerability.

Love is an open state of being through which our soul and spiritual sensitivity and consciousness can freely reach out and develop; it is the evolved state and nature we come to live by as our old defensive animal instincts are broken down and dissolved. Love opens us up from within so that we come to sense and feel the spirit and nature of all that we relate to (not just other people) and the overwhelming emotional experience is in many respects indescribable, it is something we can only share in our openness. In its early stages love may leave us feeling vulnerable, and we may fluctuate between the desire to reach out and connect and the stubborn self-defensiveness to cut off and turn our backs. Hate is a self-initiated force in direct opposition to love. It is the wilful force we use to repress and try and close up our hearts, denying love its pathway. It is intensely painful, like cutting off a part of ourselves, which is essentially what we are doing. Hate exposes our still childish nature in relationships and is essentially futile, as once you have connected with and embraced someone or something, you can never truly lose or deny that connection; you can only really isolate yourself within your personal mind, under the illusion of separateness. In the long run there is no possible way we can hide from our evolving sensitivity and the open nature of love. As human beings it is our destiny and it will open us up and dissolve the dominant instincts of our selfish animal nature, so that we might become consciously aware of our true relationship with each other and with the Universe.

The nature of love continues to grow and evolve way beyond just our closest relationships; it is a development that eventually carries us to a state of being known as unconditional love. Here we come to take full responsibility for our life and actions and are in complete unopposed acceptance and support of all other evolving life. Unconditional love is a completely open and whole state of being and awareness that exists in communion with all life in all the Universe, allowing the creative power and energy of God to live and breathe directly through us. All fully evolved life forms and entities exist in this state of being, to share with, guide and support the evolving Universe, and it is the nature of unconditional love that holds the key to the fulfilment of our own evolution on Earth. As we have developed the concept and ritual of marriage to represent the spiritually binding relationship between a man and a woman, so this concept can expand outwards to our relationship with all mankind, and eventually with the Earth and the entire Universe. We are gradually evolving towards a state of marriage with God, through our experience of life on Earth.

The true nature of love is far from weak and vulnerable, for it hides nothing of our nature and is all embracing and all exposing; love does not compromise the truth and forces us to face our deepest and darkest fears. As we grow more accustomed to and stronger in this open state of being, so our life force and spiritual entity becomes consciously aware of its eternal nature and source, transforming the nature of love to something indestructible, for you can never consciously die once you have become aware of your eternal nature.

Unconditional love is not something we can bring on or induce in our nature, it is not a case of following laws and rituals set by the example of other enlightened souls; we do not do selfless good because that is what is expected of us or because we wish to achieve some saintly status (for this is conditional), we do it because it is a natural expression of love. To exist in a state of unconditional love there are no short cuts, we each must find our own ways and work through our own nature to create our own unique bond with God. We each must experience both the pain and joy of being turned inside out: the pain of having to uncover, work through and release all our fears, negative actions and greedy selfish instincts..., and the joy of spiritual self-discovery, experienced in the overwhelming energy and emotion of the state of being and communion that is unconditional love. In love we actually feel the power of the Universal will carrying and directing our every move. We have no need to rush for the prize, as it is for the experience along the way that we have come here. All things in the Universe eventually reach their destination, we can never be separate from or masters of our evolution, we are but its expression and its fulfilment.

Light

The light radiance from a star, that is the entire spectrum of electromagnetic radiation and heat, and not just the visible spectrum of light, is a type of intelligence. It is a carrier for the creative blue prints and ideas formed within the potential energy of the vortices of a star system. Light is a pure form and source of kinetic energy, that can act both as waves and as particles: it may radiate and travel as pure uninterrupted waves of varying frequencies, and then, as it interacts with and forms matter, so its energy can be directly absorbed or dispersed into particles that are used for the structure and evolution of that particular creation. Light is the original positive energy source of all Universal life, and all light and matter comes into being through the open hole and transformer known as a star. It is the radiance and interconnected reality of light (its energy radiation), flowing between all stars and life forms, that makes up the entire network of Universal language and communication.

Scientifically we look at light and study it so much on a physical level, we have been unable to understand and appreciate, as of yet, its full life and nature. Light in its whole nature is a being, with consciousness and intelligence, as well as having measurable physical properties. To understand the full nature of light and how it exists and works in creation, the analogy of a film projector offers a good comparison that our minds can grasp and visualise.

The film projector works by shining a constant source of light through the moving frames of film, to be focused by a lens onto a screen as a motion picture that is lifelike. Now if we look at the source of energy for this light as the potential energy of spirit, which is Universal and infinite, and the lens to focus this light out into creation (to be the motion picture) as a star, then the film that dictates how the creation plays out, is the conscious blue print within the vortices. In this way light is projecting out the three-dimensional holographic image that we know and experience as creation (although to many of us, while we identify ourselves with the physical world and our personal mind, this is what we see as the 'real' world of chance and coincidence). Whatever is first imprinted within the conscious energy of the vortices is carried through the light out into space, to be constructed and played out, and this on-going motion picture of experience, exposes the full nature of light and how it plays out our creative experience.

We are the living light, in body, mind, soul, and spirit; as both source and being this is God, the Universal will. As souls and consciousness ourselves we can work with the Universal will that directs this creation and imprint new ideas within the vortices, that will then come to be played out. But we are only able to do this once we have freed ourselves from the selfish instincts of the physical body and its central identification with the mind of personality. Hence this is what we are learning to do here on Earth, so that we may become the consciousness and centre to a new star system and a new projection and experience of creation. We eventually will be able to create our own blue prints within the imaginative ether of God's infinity and thus create and become our own star system as beings of light.

Every existent form and being, from the largest star to the smallest particle, radiates its own unique energy, which is a kind of genetic energy print: it contains the knowledge and information for the entire composition and experience of that being: from its origin, to its present state and onto its future direction and potential. When you look up at a star, you are looking up at a unique form and being of creation that has consciousness and awareness, and as you connect with its light, so it is radiating and communicating its entire experience and reality.

This radiation and interaction of light energy is how the Universe remains in constant communication and balance, for all energy radiation is directed by consciousness. Science has calculated that the speed of light through a vacuum, taken from a source at point A to reach a specified distance at point B, is approximately 299,792,458 m per sec. But this relates only to the physical nature of light. In its totality light has consciousness and intelligence, and when you connect with the light radiations emanating from a star (or any being or form for that matter), then you instantaneously connect and communicate with its consciousness, regardless of the relative distance between you.

We are today still in the early stages of understanding the true nature and properties of light and its many intelligent energy radiations. If you only look to measure the physical properties then this is all you will see and come to understand. But inseparable from these properties is consciousness, and it is only through the growing sensitivity of our own consciousness that we will ever begin to communicate with and thus understand and appreciate light in its totality. Some examples as to our growing sensitivity are exposed through telepathy, clairvoyance, ESP and pyschometry. Or on a more mundane level, by the fact that we can at times pick up on the energy and mood radiating from a person without actually talking to them. But such a subtle sensitivity has a long way to go before we can directly communicate with and clearly translate the energy radiations of stars.

Astronomers, who study the properties of stars and their positions relative to Earth, have used the energy radiation's coming from the Universe and its stars (mainly light spectrums and radio waves) for some time, to distinguish them and understand their composition. As we become more sensitive and more able to record other energy radiations, so we will come to realise that this is actually an intelligent communication. As our sensitivity and awareness expands, so we ourselves will become beings of light, directly communicating and interacting with other life forms and star systems.

<u>Healing</u>

As human beings we can contract and experience many different types of illnesses, diseases and afflictions. This helps to strengthen our genetic diversity, to bind us with our environment and be aware of our physical limitations, to maintain the natural balance of populations and ecosystems, and to create challenges and obstacles to our health and evolution, that ultimately serve to draw forward greater potential and to encourage the creation of new ideas from experience. These blockages in our health can come to manifest on several different levels, each of which represents a particular body of energy and awareness that affects and interacts with every other body. There are four main bodies, each representing a specific range of energy frequencies that relates to a specific aspect of our nature: physical..., emotional..., mental..., spiritual... From the lowest frequency to the highest, each consecutive body encompasses the last. With no specific boundaries, other than the form of our physical body, the energy radiance of each body merges into the next:

At the base level there is the physical body with its entire human biology..: this can be affected by illness, disease and injury...

Encompassed about the physical is the emotional aura and body of awareness..: this is tied into the electrical pathways of our nervous system and made up of the energy emanations of our personal feelings, moods and sensitivity. This can be affected by emotional imbalances such as depression, frustration, fear and anger...

Expanding beyond the emotional is the mental or conscious body of awareness..: this is tied into the neurology of the brain and composes our personal mind and its relationship with the collective and Universal minds. Upon this level we can think, imagine, visualise, make decisions as to our direction in life, communicate with our higher mind, and make journeys into other personal or collective states of mind (for all things are connected through consciousness). It is also the place where negative thought patterns, phobias, subconscious breakdowns and mental illness can develop...

And encompassing all bodies of awareness is our spiritual nature, the link between our temporal bodies and the infinite body of Universal energy..: this is the energy and awareness of our evolved entity from which originates all the seeds of our continued evolution and personal experience. It is the level at which we are in complete communion with the Universal will and all other life. The spiritual level does not actually experience disease as such, as these manifest on the other three levels [physical, emotional and mental], but it is from here that the opening and reasoning to all illness originates: if our personal awareness becomes ignorant to, or distanced from its true soul nature and direction, or if there is a specific experience we need to go through to learn more about life, then illness, disease or imbalance can manifest and draw our attention.

All illnesses, diseases and injuries are learning experiences; they expose and teach us of our vulnerabilities and weaknesses, of the delicate balance of our evolving nature and the subsequent need to respect life. They also help us to build strength and awareness where the original weaknesses were exposed. It is through the experience of illness that we learn to heal, grow and adapt. All levels interact with and affect each other, depending on the seriousness of the illness: while a common cold may only subtly affect our emotional and mental states, a serious mental illness can profoundly alter our emotional state and make us much more vulnerable to physical illness and disease.

The manifestation of disease and illness is also part of our self-regulating nature, helping us to adapt and direct our awareness and attention to where it is needed. If we abuse our health in any way then an illness can develop and we are forced to take responsibility for our actions. There is also nature's self-regulation, which can develop disease to maintain the balance of its cycles and ecosystems, in terms of specific populations. This in turn, as regards human beings and all evolving life, increases our own genetic diversity, adaptability and resistance to disease.

As all bodies and levels of awareness affect each other and are completely interconnected, so it is that all levels of healing and treatment need to co-operate and support each other, to be most effective and bring about the best results. The deepest and most profound experience of healing takes place on the spiritual level, in what we come to learn about ourselves and why an illness developed. As the spiritual is where the reason originates for why an illness develops and comes to manifest on the physical, emotional and mental levels, so it is where the root of all healing lies, as we come to fulfil the learning experience and consciously appreciate or subconsciously accept the reasons why. Illness on any level represents an obstruction to the natural flow of our evolving spirit and its free expansion and expression. It is like a blockage in a pipeline, and to be able to heal, so the blockage must be contacted and removed. Every time we experience a potential downfall and blockage to our evolution, so we learn how to adapt and work through it and thus move beyond; both individually and collectively our experience progresses in this manner.

There are many reasons why an illness is contracted and develops. Some are very simple, like the fact that we did not protect ourselves against the cold weather or we have over consumed and abused our physical bodies. While others can be highly complex, leading back to the experiences and unresolved emotions of past lives. All have a cause, reason and purpose that can be traced and contacted if it is so required to be able to heal.

Say for example a person was to develop an extremely bad mental illness and block, which was then to affect their emotional nature and make them extremely depressed and demotivated, as well as draining their vitality and diminishing their weight and physique through lack of care and appetite. The illness is like a weed: it is deeply rooted in its original reason (abuse, traumatic experience, past life actions, for example), but comes to grow and develop through the other bodies and more into everyday life. If we were just to treat the physical symptoms because we could not see or did not understand the depth of its origin, then it would be just like chopping off the head of the weed. The physical problems may recover for a while, but as the root remains, then the head may grow through again, and the same or other physical and emotional symptoms would return.

For healing to be complete, then we have to dig to find the problem, no matter how deep, and the person with the illness has to want to take responsibility for their own healing, to gain the spiritual experience that truly resolves the problem. It is no good to give up responsibility and expect someone else to do the work for you, to hand over the magic pill and give you all the answers and reasons. Without direct personal involvement and experience, the block cannot be removed or will only remanifest in some way. While this spiritual healing takes place, in tracing, facing up to and working through the psychological block, so this can be co-operatively supported with healing on all other levels, according to what has developed: emotional counselling and support and medical treatment and advice for example. As the spiritual lesson is learnt and the person comes to take full responsibility for their life again, so this reflects on all other levels: increased mental stability, a return of motivation and emotional well being, and better health and physical vitality. It is certainly not always an easy process or experience, and those providing support need steadfast patience and stamina. However deep the roots and however far back they go in time, goes some way to defining how much work, time and effort is needed; it can take a lifetime, or even longer in some cases.

If we take a close look at how illness, disease and injury comes to affect a person's life, thinking and attitudes; the conflicts that may arise and subsequent changes in perspective, and how it effects those close to them (family, friends, carers, doctors), then we can begin to appreciate its reasoning: why we choose these experiences and how they are working to help us to learn and grow as human beings.

Say as another example a person develops a fatal illness such as cancer, at a very early age and for no consciously apparent reason. This will come to affect the person's family and loved ones as much as it does themselves. There may be much soul searching and a need to find an answer as to why. There may be some anger and frustration, which, as it is released, may lead to a greater acceptance of life and a greater openness and honesty between family and friends that strengthens their love. Perspectives and priorities to life may change, there may be depression and a lack of will to go on, doctors may say there is nothing that can be done, which might spark a deeper search for healing and a determination to find other approaches, which in rare cases can lead to the recession and curing of cancer..., or a person may just focus upon the sharing and intimacy with friends and family for the remainder of the time they have left.

The person with cancer and those close to him or her, may all have to face a deeper inner confrontation with the idea of death and mortality. They may have to witness the person they care for physically degenerate and die, over a long period of time, and the example of how that person goes through this, can help to transform our fears of death and change our outlook on life. Again every case is unique in its reasons and affects, and rather than look from a fearful perspective with a desperate need to cling to life (even though we may have to face the deep and painful personal loss of a loved one), if we were to look a little deeper, then we would begin to see the immense potential for growth and learning that such experiences can offer.

For every body of energy and level of awareness there is a different general approach to healing and treatment, although healing on any particular level will help and support healing on every other level. The co-operation of these approaches offers a wholistic view to healing that could carry our potential to heal way beyond its present reality. This is in fact already beginning to happen and spread through our collective consciousness. Of course all the practitioners of healing have to be genuine and have an in-depth knowledge and experience of their chosen field:

i) The Physical body:

For the physical body we have developed and evolved a whole institution and library of experience to draw from. Over many years and generations our knowledge of the physical body has been expanded, thanks to the dedication of many lives. The medicine and technology we have today would astound and probably frighten the people of a thousand years ago. They would see it as something alien and probably hail it as something miraculous from God, or even the Devil. Trial and error, research and extensive documentation has led us to our present reality, where we have extremely highly trained doctors, nurses and physicians who have a wealth of understanding as to the biology and physiology of the human body (as well as those of plants and animals, according to their chosen fields). They have a wealth of treatments to aid our natural healing processes.

Where doctors can sometimes lack is in their cold approach to patients (which is understandable when you realise their focus is almost entirely on the mechanics of the body), and this can at times create more trauma and problems for patients who have to completely put their lives in another persons hands. Sometimes their personal judgements and opinions can also be damaging and small minded: they may feel superior due to the immense time and effort they have put into becoming qualified, and in this respect they may dismiss and deny the effectiveness of other types of healing, or they may give the impression they understand an illness (psychological or emotional in its origin) which they do not, and advise treatments with drugs that can actually increase problems and disassociation.

Doctors have been known to tell people who trust them that there is nothing that can be done, when in fact there are many other approaches to healing that could help. The problems with doctors are not altogether common and many of the smaller minded approaches are being broken down and opened up through experience. Part of the problem also lies in the patients approach, as many people look for the quickest and easiest way out and give away their responsibility. They look up to the doctor as a miracle worker and expect answers and immediate cures. Ultimately doctors are there to advise and on the whole do a fantastic job in their field of expertise, which should be respected but not over estimated. We as the patient need to take more responsibility and to retain our intuition, to speak up if something we are told does not feel right. We must remember that doctors are human the same as anyone else, and they can at times make mistakes and certainly do not have all the answers.

ii) The Emotional body:

The emotional body has an aura (energy emanation) that extends beyond the boundaries of our physical body. This connects and communicates with our surroundings and with the people that we relate to and sensually perceive. When problems arise in our emotional body and aura, we have trained counsellors and carers available to help, again with a vast knowledge of the human emotional nature at their disposal. People who work as carers are usually part trained, but to do their job well they need to be naturally empathic and sympathetic, to be able to connect with a persons emotional state, and such gifts usually come from personal experience. Probably one of the greatest sources of emotional healing and support is the love of our friends and family, although these relationships can also be one of the biggest causes of emotional pains.

On this level a carer helps to put someone at ease, so that they can accept and express their feelings more freely and to feel that they are valued and respected. Feelings can be traced and clarified as they are brought out into the open and the carer acts as a sturdy mooring and support for the expression of our more uncontrollable and upsetting emotions, often feeding back a more objective view that can help a person to understand and come to terms with their feelings and experiences.

Again there are dangers and mistakes can be made, although it helps us to learn and progress in the long run. People can feel extremely vulnerable and volatile when they open themselves up and expose their feelings. Situations can be delicate and need to be handled with care; judgements and pressured advice delivered in a brash and out spoken way, can leave scars and create more problems. Carers cannot take it upon themselves to resolve other people's emotional problems, they themselves have to do the work to heal and make changes. A carer supports and guides the process of release to help a person find their own answers and resolutions, offering open advice or suggestions only if necessary. It is very important that the person with the problem makes the decisions as to what to say and do, so that any actions and changes will sustain themselves and grow according to their own will. The act of crying is in itself one of the greatest and most common forms of emotional release.

iii) The Mental body:

Again the mental, or conscious body, emanates and interacts beyond the emotional. We have our individual minds that relate to and reflect our personal experiences, and this then extends to link in with the collective mind of humanity, and beyond to that of the Universe. Problems within the conscious body, or mind, tend to be the most deep rooted and disruptive, and to help with the healing of the mind, we have trained psychotherapists and psychoanalysts. Again personal exploration and experience of the human mind and psyche is all important to understanding psychology. We might be able to recognise and learn certain common patterns and reactions of the mind from books and studies, but the constructions and interactions of the conscious, subconscious and collective conscious minds are unique in each individual, and to be able to venture into these states of mind requires a certain degree of personal experience and exploration.

Psychological healing is very similar and strongly connected to the emotional, and involves the uncovering, experience of and expression of thoughts and feelings that lie at the root of the problem. The difference with the psychotherapist is that they are more able to enter into the mind of another person, and sometimes uncover things within the subconscious that a person has not been able to contact or face on their own. Again it can be an extremely delicate operation, and the subconscious fabric of the mind has to be treated with the greatest of respect and sometimes needs support in its rebuilding over long periods of time.

Cases that involve interferences from the collective conscious and subconscious (the hearing of voices, schizophrenia, possession, for example), require great depths of mental strength and understanding on the psychotherapist's part; to be able to enter into those states of mind and retain stability, as they endeavour to guide the person who is stuck back to their own consciousness. This is why few psychologists actually venture that far at present and why there is still very little collective understanding as to the nature of such mental illnesses. There are many theories as to the cause and nature of such illnesses, but only the personal experience of entering into these states of mind can reveal truthful answers and understanding, and enable effective guidance and healing by the psychotherapist to this depth. There is a great deal of work involved in psychological healing and still an immense amount for us to learn and explore, but just because we do not yet understand the reasons behind certain more profound mental illnesses, does not mean that there are no cures for them: there is a cure for every problem and affliction, for it is just a case of restoring balance. We will only discover the path to certain cures, when we are willing to dig deep enough and give enough time and energy to work through it.

iv) The Spiritual body:

The spiritual body represents all the levels of our awareness that lie beyond the tangible states of our physical, emotional and mental energies. Each extension of sensitivity and awareness has a more profound influence over the previous ones: for example, a person with a severe mental illness who is treated only on a physical level, may physically improve for a while, but their emotional and mental states will show little improvement or relapse after showing small signs of improvement. Whereas if they are treated on a mental level, the true root and cause of the illness can be contacted, brought forward and resolved, and the effects on the emotional and physical states will naturally begin to clear and re-balance.

A spiritual healer works in a much more wholistic and complete way to stimulate and support healing on every level: physical, emotional, mental and spiritual. As they connect with the consciousness and being of a person, so they can begin to feel and draw forward a clear understanding of the nature of their spiritual evolution. They appreciate that there are needs and reasons behind any illness or imbalance that develops, and that the self-regulating nature of spirit, means that the person has to open themselves up and go through whatever experience is necessary to enable their own healing.

A true spiritual healer exists in a completely open state of being, a state of unconditional love, and while they have individuality and personality, they are carried and directed by the Universal will and the developing needs of the evolving life about them; these things become their needs and feelings. They make no claim and accept no responsibility to having healed a person, as they know the person themselves has to be responsible: they have to acknowledge their problem and seek out help, they have to lay themselves open and face and release the block, and they have everything to gain and learn from the experience.

A spiritual healer uncompromisingly supports this natural process. They have the natural ability and sight to see and feel the needs of a person and the reasons for their problems, and they can impart this direct connection and sight upon the person who needs healing, so that they are put back in touch with themselves and can experience a sense of wholeness and well being. This can then help to clarify the problem and releases and stimulates their own natural healing. It is as if the spiritual healer gives the person a reflection of their own spiritual power and potential, connecting them up with the Universe and giving them a true perspective of their spiritual nature. This experience then brings forward and activates whatever realisations and healing is required. How the healer imparts this to the person is unique to their own soul and its path of realisation and enlightenment; there is no learning or format to spiritual healing, it evolves naturally from our own life experience. Spiritual healing cannot be induced or learnt from texts, it is a completely natural process that emanates from the experience and enlightenment of the soul.

A person who has experienced healing in this manner may look up to the healer or feel beholden to them (which can happen in any form of healing), due to the profundity of the experience. It is like an evolutionary boost, exposing our whole nature and making everything clear for a moment, and then returning us to ourselves to work through and release the problem. Any genuine spiritual healer would make it clear that they have only exposed what already belonged to the person themselves, and have done what comes naturally to them. We often look at such healing in a state of awe, although many people today might not even believe it to be real, unless they were personally involved in such an experience. We can mistakenly associate this awe with the personality of the healer, when what we are really in awe of, is our own potential and nature yet to be realised.

A spiritual healer is following and reacting to their own needs and instincts (to grow in communion with the Universe and learn how to serve as its creative expression) in exactly the same way that the person who seeks healing is following their needs. We work and exist on different levels according to our awareness, and thus support and carry each other: without the need to be healed there would be no spiritual healer and neither soul could learn or progress in this way. In this respect, circumstances and situations are created in the Universal mind and brought about by our souls, specifically to increase learning and awareness. We all equally have a part to play, and who knows what new ideas may develop from such experiences.

Spiritual healers and enlightened beings are usually rare, as many move beyond incarnation on the Earth, and the few that do come back, do so to help us evolve collectively. There are usually just enough to excite our curiosity and keep us venturing forward and questioning. Many live ordinary lives and pass relatively unnoticed, as their state of awareness is as ordinary to them as ours is to us, but they do much to stimulate and open up our collective consciousness just by being here and being themselves.

There are many people around the world today who practice what has been called spiritual healing, and yet in the majority of cases this is more a channelled form of emotional healing rather then genuine spiritual healing. That is not to say that it does not affect the spiritual level, as it will have its affect on every level and helps to teach all who are involved. But misunderstandings and problems can manifest through this type of healing, especially when the healer wishes to take responsibility for a healing and leaves the person healed feeling obligated. Emotional healing that is portrayed as spiritual healing (via the laying on of hands for example) works when the person performing the healing opens themselves up to connect with the person being healed. They may lay their hands on them or hold them just off the person's body, or they may have some other way or ritual to achieve this connection. They then act as an open medium for energy that passes through them into the emotional aura of the person being healed and on to the places in need of healing, in the physical, emotional and mental bodies.

Many good results have and do come from this type of healing, and in a lot of cases the act of seeking out this type of spiritual healing and opening yourself up to the possibility, possibly after being passed around the established medical system and against personal scepticism, is the experience that allows self-healing to take place. In this way the spiritual or emotional healers are the ones that advertise and advocate this possibility to our collective consciousness, and rather than being personally responsible for an individuals healing they encourage and support the natural process. Of course not all healings are successful: there is often a genuine need for a person to acknowledge or experience something within themselves before healing can become complete. This is why healing cannot be forced upon a person; they must first come to the point where they feel they need it and actually want to be healed.

As greed is still a part of our human nature, then there are some people out there who proclaim themselves to be masters and healers whose main priority is making money through deceit. They are confidence tricksters who charge ridiculous sums for simple techniques that have little affect. Of course in time their record will be their own undoing, but this is another reason why taking personal responsibility for healing is all-important. Sadly it is those who wish to take least responsibility that are most susceptible to being used, conned or abused, and these are often the cases the media latch onto and expose.

This is a sign of our times though, and proves that this sort of healing is becoming popular, for if it were not, then the money makers of our world would not gravitate towards it. We should try to remember however, that such cases are a minority and are part of the leaning process. We should always trust and use our own instinct and intuition when seeking healing; if what somebody is offering us or asking from us does not feel right, then we can always move on and look elsewhere. Taking responsibility for the self is the primary and most important action in any form of healing. While healing can be encouraged and supported on many different levels, by different people and practices, we are the only ones that can truly initiate it, and sustain our natural balance and health once it is complete.

Again this is just a general outline of how I have experienced healing and a personal expression of what I believe it involves. Every thought, feeling and action we project conveys energy, and regardless of how large or small the amount may be, this can be used to help to affect change and healing in a positive way for what ever it is directed towards: be it a person, animal, plant, community, ecosystem or the planet as a whole. All levels of healing and treatment have something to offer, and in co-operation they can be miraculously effective. None of them really need to dominate or speak out against another if healing is truly the ultimate priority. This merely exposes the arrogant opinions of certain practitioners that are destined to die out in the light of more open-minded thinking. The development of every illness and disease on what ever level, is unique to the experience of the individual, and in this lies the key to all healing: what is paramount to our healing in every respect, is the responsibility we take for ourselves and the openness and willingness we have to learn and to heal.

Part 2

Evolution

A Brief Insight Into Human Evolution

The past is cast in stone;
the present, created now, is modelled upon the face
of the past,
and the future, with all its possibilities,
is the clay within our hands.

All of these are one continual stream,
flowing one to the next:
past, present, future;
whose destination is assured,
in the Ocean from whence they came.

It has always been my main aim and motivation in writing to try to simplify and convey ideas and concepts in a commonly tangible way. To trim away the complexities of specialised science and traditional religion that seem to alienate so many people from even contemplating certain ideas or following particular trains of thought...., and in doing so, to help to dissolve the many fears, superstitions and rhetorical texts that have restricted free thinking in our cultures and societies throughout our more recent history. I am aware that in the entirety of its experience, our evolution and recorded history to date is a very complex subject and living reality, with so many lives, cultures and civilisations. Likewise I am aware of the great wealth of knowledge and theories that exist, both scientific and religious, thanks to the dedication of many lifetimes past and present. All of these can lay claim in some part, to both our welfare and advancement as a race, as well as to our downfall at times. And yet, with no disrespect to what any culture, religion or science has given to us, the more time and energy you pour into something, and the more detailed or specific your research or rituals become, then the more complexities and divisions can be written in and created.

With this in mind, I know that there is absolutely no truth in the idea that a life long scholar of say, astrophysics, astronomy or religious text (for example), is any more qualified to speak of the nature and reasoning of the Universe, than any other human being alive today. While their minds may be more accustomed to pondering upon the nature of the Universe, the knowledge of such scholars is much more about the history of what has been said, done, and written to date, within their chosen fields, than it actually is about the nature of life and creation. The Universe flows through and carries us all equally, offering its wisdom without judgement and with only one prerequisite...., that of an open mind.

The Collective Mind

To appreciate how human beings have evolved consciously beyond their previous animal nature, and to see and understand the general direction that this evolution has taken, we need to take a few steps back to be able to view the human race as one collective being and mind:

All states of being that have a common identity (animal, vegetable, mineral, or in this case human), indeed anything with a form of identity, has its own collective conscious and subconscious mind of experience. This collective mind, much like the human individual mind, represents the entire energy imprints of experience to date and the future potential for its continued evolution, according to its particular identity or race. The collective conscious represents the total spectrum of the present awareness and reality of any particular race or identity, according to the sum awareness of all its living individuals. While the collective subconscious is what borders and encapsulates the conscious: beneath the conscious it is a record of all previous experience that has now evolved to become inherent and instinctual (the instinctive subconscious), while above the conscious it is the veil and medium through which all future potential can be channelled into real experience and become living consciousness (the spiritual subconscious).

I have defined and used the term subconscious here, as opposed to the unconscious, as I believe all things to be composed of consciousness and therefore never truly unconscious. Even the most inbred instinctual behavioural impulses are accessible through consciousness. In this way the conscious mind gradually ascends in its awareness, as revelations gradually become our instinctual behaviour, and mankind becomes more enlightened to its source, identity and place within the Universe. Every human being has a part to play, adding to and furthering the collective experience.

All the individuals of a particular identity or race are connected to the collective mind, they compose it, and whatever one or more individuals comes to experience, learn or realise, is then made available through the collective mind to the whole race. Or to look at it from the other side, from the Universe's perspective: as new experiences and insights are made available by the Universe to a particular race, to advance their evolution according to their needs, so the most open and sensitive minds touch and expose this first (in their own unique way), and gradually it is worked down to encompass the whole of the race and to eventually become a living inherent reality.

As regards the human race this collective mind is self-regulating: changing, moving and adapting, according to the needs of its evolutionary directives, and it is from this perspective that I will be looking to go on to explore the actions, reactions and general direction of our more recent evolution as a race. You can clearly see a pattern emerge in our recent evolution, as our relationship with the Universe (God) continues to open and develop. New ideas and realisations are first introduced by the individual (visionaries, saints, philosophers, inspired scientists..), and then become more and more accepted and part of our collective reality, to eventually become a way of life. We still look up to many of these names and hold them aloft in our collective mind, for what they first showed to us and their unique way of presenting this. And yet what we really look up to, maybe without even realising it, is the open and free state of mind that allowed these people to touch upon such ideas in the first place. Such a state of mind is what our present evolution compels us toward; those that showed us true vision, were only exposing what was on its way down to us all, and doing what came naturally to them.

With this framework of our collective states of mind: the conscious, bordered by the instinctive subconscious and spiritual subconscious, what follows is an attempt to outline the basic direction of our evolution as a race. Like a river our consciousness is fluid as it moves forward through time: turning and twisting according to the lie of the land, building up behind and breaking down barriers, flooding and splitting as it follows many different paths..., all of which eventually lead to the ocean.

Translating The Legends And Stories Of The Past

The Fall From Grace

Our most physical genetic origins in the Earth lie in our animal nature, and to understand our nature in the present, how our consciousness has evolved beyond this nature and why we are presently prone to experience conflict within ourselves as a race, we first need to appreciate the base instincts of our animal natures. Animals have three main evolutionary directives, all of which relate to each other and serve the progression and genetic diversity of the fertile Earth, which is part of their purpose within creation. These directives are: self-preservation and survival, reproduction, and adaptation to the environment. They are for the most part competitive and selfish to produce stability, durability and flexibility within the naturally balanced and self-regulating ecosystems animals inhabit. Although there are many cases of co-operation and co-existence, these exist primarily due to each species instinct of self-preservation. Animals for the most part live from the instinctive subconscious where these directives are ongoing, and here lies the basic root instincts of our own human nature, which are now being challenged, broken down, and superseded, as we evolve through the spiritual subconscious.

I experience and understand all things as being conscious, from atoms, to plants, to planets, to galaxies, to God..., consciousness pervades all, although not always in a way we may allow ourselves to acknowledge and appreciate. All things are open, connected to source and interactive: some things may have the directive of conscious free will to express (which we would most readily compare and relate to), while others, say an atom for example, may be a small constituent part of a more collective consciousness that obeys more simplistic and stricter laws. All things have their purpose within creation, which is why atoms are stable building blocks and humans are highly individual adventurous souls living through a complex biological organism; they exist as part of each other.

What separated humans from animals was the introduction of new directives: namely to experience and explore individual conscious free will, and to evolve as open and enlightened spiritual entities, self-realised and unopposed to all other evolving life. These new directives were set to breakdown and will eventually replace the old animal directives as priorities for human life. This transformation from animal to spiritual consciousness and the confrontations, breakdowns and breakthroughs this has brought about in our nature, is the story of our more recent history. It is a story I hope to clarify, as we see how our consciousness has moved, changed and reacted as it follows these new directives.

As humans evolved beyond animals, they consciously began to evolve through the higher planes of our solar existence. They imposed, expressed and learnt how to direct their individual free wills to a much higher degree than animals, creating much more complex and defined personalities and egos (the impulses of the plane of Mars). They continued to project this will into every aspect of the Earth's nature: creating many extensive languages, recognising and naming animals, vegetables and minerals, travelling to and exploring new environments, reacting to and communicating with other social groups out of curiosity, respect and co-operation (as opposed to violent reactions of fear, self-preservation and survival), and developing and forming societies around pure forms of religion and stories of creation, that stemmed from a direct experience of the spirit and substance of nature, and from a sense of awe to the stars and heavens above (the impulses of the plane of Jupiter).

For some time these new impulses carried human consciousness into exploring the entirety of the Earth's nature, and to expressing the many different aspects of this growing relationship and knowledge through individual personality and tribal culture. It was a type of shamanic existence, where God was in all nature and alive, and man was now his companion and friend as opposed to his more ignorant animal subject. As of yet there was no conflict within human nature, as our impulses to evolve moved us forward unquestionably and the natural balance of the Earth and its ecosystems remained undisturbed. It truly was a state of 'Eden' with man and nature in complete harmony; the violence of nature and of man's animal instincts still existed of course, but as an unquestioned compulsion of survival that helped to maintain the balance of the ecosystems and its food chains.

Eventually, as man's impulse to explore the Earth became an inherent part of his nature and we existed in a completely conscious balance with the nature of Earth, our consciousness began to transcend to a new level of awareness; one that began to expose our physical limitations upon the Earth and thus turned our eyes and minds to the Universe and its reasoning (the impulses of the plane of Saturn and those beyond Saturn). The two opposing energies of creation (positive and negative, light and dark, creative and destructive) were exposed to our consciousness, and as we began to question our existence, we faced for the first time opposition as to the continued direction of our evolution.

As there were two directions of force within the Universe, so we had the choice of two directions in our evolution: we could either continue the expansion or be part of the implosion. The doors to the knowledge of the Universe had begun to open before us, our awareness had moved beyond just the nature of Earth, and the forces of creation were available for us to learn to master. With the gift of self-awareness and free will, the choice seemed to be ours as to which path to follow: do we progress, open and serve the Universe (God), to follow what we then termed good...? Or do we regress, turn in upon the

Earth and its nature, serve our own ego's and desires, to follow what we termed, at its most extreme, evil....?

The conflict, or battle between good and evil, had begun. Our evolutionary directives and spiritual natures, driven by the inspiration to know more, called us forward to evolve consciously beyond the Earth and serve the Universe. While our animal natures, driven more by fear, held us down and called us back to deny further evolution, to manipulate our surroundings according to our will and the needs and desires of our personal will. And we, both individually and collectively as a race, were, indeed still are, pushed and pulled between the two. So began the master plan that implemented one of the greatest lessons we have come to learn and experience as a human being: the doors to the Universe were open and the forces of creation were ours to direct, but without the understanding and responsibility to use them in harmony with the needs of nature and the Universe, the stability of creation breaks down, and physical existence, the balance of life itself, can be destroyed.

Humans became a channel for the knowledge and power of the Universe to enter the Earth's environment, raising the level of conscious energy and stimulating all evolution. The doors to the Universe are two-way, and now more highly evolved entities (spirits that may have evolved awareness through other star systems) were free to enter into human genetics and experience human nature. A great and highly evolved civilisation was gradually established, the source of the many stories of Atlantis, and this began to link the Universe directly with the Earth and tap its infinite power resources. But sadly this was a civilisation that was destined toward destruction, due to the increasing conflict in human nature and the manipulative will of the human ego. As humans were becoming open beings and were married to the Earth's nature and environment, so all the imbalances and destructive energies they introduced began to affect the Earth's balance and ecosystems, and such instabilities naturally reacted and reflected back destruction upon our environments and civilisations.

Basically this conflict is taking place within our collective consciousness as a necessity for us to experience, if we are to come to appreciate and channel the forces of creation and become aware of our true identity as spiritual beings. This is then reflected upon the surface in our individual consciousness and day-to-day reality, as we are seen to be at war with ourselves. Some individuals seem to represent good and others represent evil, while ultimately the battle is fought and won within each of us individually. Being self-regulating and guided by the Universal will, human consciousness reacted to its immediate needs to continue evolving and restore balance to the Earth's structure and nature. It devised a way to both breakdown the dominance of our animal ego natures and to clarify our responsibility in the use of the infinite resources of the Universe.

This was implemented over a period of many thousands of years and is a process that is nearing its completion in our present time. In a way the human race has been inoculated with the self-destructive diseases of greed, excess and irresponsibility, to be allowed to experience them for a time and come to appreciate their painful and destructive repercussions. Eventually we will learn from this experience that there is nothing productive to gain from following these directions, and freely choose to surrender our animal instincts and egos, to serve the Universe that has given these gifts to us. This is just a brief explanation as to how such a process was set in place within our collective consciousness and how this has then reflected in our recent history: in our legends, religions and science, and in our individual experience of ourselves.

First, the knowledge and free use of the infinite power and energy of the Universe had to be protected and concealed for a time, to limit the destructive damage our conflict was causing. Collectively our awareness had begun to establish itself upon the plane of Saturn, thus allowing individual souls to make their own progressions beyond this plane. Here we could learn to become masters of the Earth and its elemental forces, through progressive realisations as to the source and physical limitations of life, and beyond this the doors to the rest of the Universe were open and its knowledge freely available. A veil was then constructed within our consciousness to conceal this open connection to the Universe, and our awareness was gradually drawn back to the Earth.

This was reflected in natural disaster and catastrophe, as the great civilisation embodied in the idea of Atlantis collapsed, and for the most part disappeared from trace. The knowledge from this time was fractionated across the globe: it was channelled out over many generations (by those evolved beings who had come to serve the Universal will) into stories, myths, prophecies, written teachings and symbols, forms of the oracle, religious and cultural wisdoms and sites of worship, buildings and artefacts....., and much of the energy lay dormant within the crystalline formations of the Earth. As the past and what it had revealed to human consciousness could not be completely removed or wiped clear (what is done can never be undone as it is written eternally by its experience and will always have been), so the knowledge was drawn away and concealed for a time from the mainstream of human consciousness, ready to be reawakened when we had learnt our lessons of responsibility.

Upon the ground this was seen as our fall from grace, with mankind being left to feel split apart and incomplete, as if we were being punished for what we had judged to be the wrong we were doing (although in reality we were only experiencing a natural and necessary reaction to our evolutionary needs). Some evolved beings, who were consciously aware of the process that was underway, were able to support and guide it: sustaining and channelling the knowledge into teachings and stories, maintaining faith in life and encouraging the human race by their examples, working to redress the imbalances and maintain some stability upon the Earth and within human consciousness. Other evolved beings, some of which had evolved through other star systems, were corrupted and destabilised by the experience of the ego and its powerful animal instincts towards self-preservation. Some of these came to create positions of great power and be defiled as Gods: they enslaved and abused the rights of much of mankind, seeking to rule by domination and fear, and they tended to manipulate energy and their environment to fulfil personal desires and self-inflated visions, often in destructive conflict with the Earth's needs and natural balance.

The perception of the collective majority of humankind, their view of God and the Universe, was now dictated by these fearful changes and power struggles. God, or the favoured cultural idols, was thus depicted as powerful and mighty, full of wrath and vengeance: he would smite and punish those who did wrong and went against him, while caring for and delivering those who did right. This perception was of course man-made and did not represent the true nature of God; it merely reflected the experience of humankind at that time.

Although confused and in decline, humankind still had strong links and gained insights into the present direction and purpose of creation, and from these came several truths and prophecies (along with other misled or unbalanced beliefs) that helped people to appreciate why things were changing so drastically. Much of what was spoken at this time was coloured by this perception of God and written in terms of fear and might, and it is only when these elements are removed, that we can fully appreciate what was being communicated here. This period represents the time of the, 'Old Testament', and I speak of 'Testament' here as describing man's relationship with God as a whole, not just in respect of the Old Testament of the Christian Bible or Jewish tradition. Man's relationship was for the most part, one of fear and reverence: we knelt before God and looked up and begged. As we continue into the time of the, 'New Testament', so we will be able to appreciate how this relationship has changed, and what this has meant to the further evolution of humankind.

<u>The Construction Of The Abyss</u>

As our regression in awareness took place, a veil of darkness was constructed within our collective consciousness that acted to conceal the knowledge and power of the Universe from us for a time. This veil, known as the Abyss or bottomless pit (names given to it at a time when there was obviously much fear as to what was happening), is an amazing construction that reflects completely our needs to evolve and learn responsibility. The Abyss is an illusionary barrier of darkness between our Earthly consciousness of physical mortality, personality and ego, and our spiritual consciousness of the Universe and its infinite energy resources. It acts to separate the two so that our Earthly consciousness can pass through the real experience it needs to learn responsibility. We are kept within its boundaries to experience, expose and eventually exorcise the potentially destructive elements of our nature, while the Universe outside is left relatively undisturbed by these destabilising experiences.

Individually and thus collectively we each must face and pass through the Abyss to reunite our complete nature, and to gain the awareness of our eternal spiritual nature and the Universe this may come to serve. The darkness of the Abyss reflects back to each of us the weaknesses and fears of our own egos. It is an illusory barrier that we compose by the fears we project, and on the other side lies our spiritual awareness that works to compel us forward and through ('calling' us forward).

Nothing in time stands still, so if we do not progress, then what we build may stagnate and begin to disintegrate. Evolution inspires and compels us to progress and offers the only true steps forward, and to cross the Abyss, as we cannot see beyond and receive no guarantees, we have only faith in this heart felt inspiration to take those steps. To cross the Abyss we are compelled to surrender our animal instincts of self-preservation, face and relinquish our fears, and step into the unknown with no guarantees of where this may lead or even if we shall survive or pass through...., and all we have to trust and have faith in, is that one simple impulse and need to progress.

It is like being compelled to go on a quest for self-discovery and truth, and then coming to the edge of a chasm. You know you have to go forward to succeed, yet the fall before you is dark and bottomless. Fear (the voice of your self-preserving animal nature and rational mind) imagines all the horrors that may lie in that darkness and begs you to turn back to the places and way of life that you know, using any means to justify fear. The evolutionary and soul's need to know truth and purpose, and to discover our real identity and nature, that compels us on and will not allow us to rest (the calling of your spiritual nature and awareness), tells you that the darkness is just an illusion and that there is a way through in front of you. If you choose to trust this voice, as opposed to that of fear, you will be able to walk forward and cross to the other side, to reach the answers that await and realise your true potential. This is the real step of faith that acts to transform our primary instincts, and I can share from experience, that once you take those wholehearted steps into the unknown, to lay your life on the line, then the darkness dissolves completely and the truth is revealed.

When you look at this anecdote you can see where the idea of the bottomless pit came from; yet it describes perfectly the mental and emotional experience of what evolution has brought us to face within our consciousness. Upon the ground, all human experience throughout this time in history is geared to carrying us to face and eventually cross the Abyss; from the mundane day-to-day routines, to the most profound revelations. Internally by conscience and karma we are learning and judging for ourselves and preparing to take those steps. There is no other judge: did we trust, step forward and follow our heart and do what felt 'right'...?, or did we turn away in fear, strike out and take for ourselves, and do what felt 'wrong' on reflection? These judgements are for ourselves alone to pronounce and learn from.

Our developing conscience is the voice of our spiritual nature directing the way ahead, and what we each adhere to individually thus reflects collectively in the laws and societies of our time. The more individuals that adhere to their conscience and follow their heartfelt intuition as opposed to their fears, then the more this way of life is supported for the whole human race, and so our destructive tendencies begin to die away. The real inner experience of following conscience, putting behind us the selfish fears of survival, and stepping wholeheartedly forward into the unknown, carries us across the Abyss and displaces the old animal priority instincts with new priorities of faith, love and spiritual intuition. This then exposes the knowledge and nature of the Universe and of the eternal 'life' of our conscious spiritual entities, so that balance is restored and we can move on to the rest of the Universe and beyond in our own evolution. There is no way around this, for in time we each must face our fears and the repercussions of our actions, to be able to evolve beyond them. Only by carrying the light of real experience forward into the unknown, can we come to cross and dissolve the darkness of the Abyss, and thus become whole again.

<u>The Exposure Of Christ</u>

As our regression in awareness slowed and became complete, and the dark veil of the Abyss was gradually constructed within the fabric of our collective consciousness, so we approached a definite turning point in this process of learning and transformation. Our relationship with God, our awareness of the Universe and its progressively evolving nature, had become weak and disjointed. In many respects we had lost sight of our true purpose and direction in life as a race, and just maintained a living as best we could. Our connection to the Universe was now much less intuitive and direct, depending on the oracles, teachings, religious laws and rituals that had been created, written and passed down during the generations of the regression. These being maintained and upheld by the religious orders and groups of this period in history, that were scattered about the world. Our view of God reflected our more recent experience of life on Earth, which had become unstable and full of hardships. Thus God was portrayed as being vengeful, full of wrath and power, rewarding only the righteous. This was of course purely a childish man-made perspective of the nature of God and the Universe, but one that dominated many of the religions of this time.

There were some religions and groups of individuals within this period, scattered across the globe, that were dedicated to maintaining conscious links with the Universe and to understanding and guiding the changes at hand. Some of these could be found in the cultures of Egypt and Africa, the Americas, Greece, India, China, Indonesia, the European Celts and Druids, the Hebrews and Essenes. All about the world there were people working, mostly behind-the-scenes, for the collective good of mankind. These were successful to a greater or lesser degree, according to how dogmatic their rituals and literature became and how literally later generations took their stories, myths, and prophecies. Many of these connections to the Universe became coloured and distorted, hence the perceptions of a God / or Gods of war, punishment and vengeance, alongside the Gods of creativity that first gave life to humans. If however we look at the basic themes of some of these teachings and prophecies, by translating out some of the religious and cultural language and perceptions, it becomes easy to see the similarities in what they were trying to relate.

Some of what I have written, and will go on to write about in this book, can at times be identified with the books of the Bible and many of the Christian religions, although many of the themes occur in other religious texts and traditions. The Christian Bible is a fairly jumbled collection of stories, teachings and prayers: the source of the Old Testament is the 39 books of the Jewish bible originally written in Hebrew (with a little in Aramaic), plus the addition of a further 7 books by Roman Catholics, some of which was originally written in Greek. The New Testament, also originally written in Greek, relates the life of Jesus, the early establishment of the Christian faith and a book of prophetic revelations.

Viewed anthropologically it gives an excellent reflection of the changes in man's perception of God: God, the creative life force and intelligence, was personified by man as the father of humankind, watching over us, intervening if necessary. This made the concept of God approachable to all people. Even though it was usually only a few select scholars of religion, or prophets, that acted as the voice of God, people could talk to the father image of God in prayer, and at times hear his answer in their minds or through miraculous signs. But such a God was often portrayed as above us and beyond our reach, looking down, controlling and commanding his children. That was of course until the New Testament began and with it a new message and perception of God, one where God was shown to exist within us and comes to be revealed as our hearts (the central energy of our identity and nature) are opened in the true nature of love.

The Bible is a hotchpotch of historical fact, story telling and parable, inspired writings and prayer, prophecy and over zealous religious fantasy. Far from being the unquestionable word of God, it is quite simply man's word about his experience, understanding and belief in God, and how God affects and interacts with our lives and evolution. It should be remembered that over many centuries there have been many omissions and additions to the Bible, according to the compatibility of language translations and the currently favoured religious ideals of the time.

On the whole it has bared up fairly well to the passing of time, and when viewed impartially from a distance, it exposes a basic theme of transition: First there is the foundations of the metaphysical creation, man's fall from grace and his early relationship with God and the Universe, and the establishment and history of the Jewish nation with the promise of salvation through the birth of a saviour...Then there is a distinct turning point, due mainly to the birth of Jesus and the exposure of the nature of Christ (something that funnily enough is not recognised by much of the Jewish orthodox church). This leads to the spreading of a new idea of God, the establishment of Christianity and the future promise of a return of Christ at such a time when man was deemed ready, having exposed on Earth all the realities of his greedy animal nature.

This common theme, of a fall from grace, the birth of a prophet and turning point, future judgement and reward, runs throughout many of the world's religions and beliefs. They relate God's supposed dissatisfaction with humankind and his behaviour: God is said to be angry, punishing the bad, wiping out bad cities and peoples, forcing them to beg forgiveness. This at least was man's reasoning for what was happening in the world.

If we liberate this idea of the judgements of time and culture, then what is actually being related here is a breakdown in man's relationship with the flow of his evolution and his consciousness of the Universe. This represents mankind's regression in awareness, as evolution counteracts mankind's inner conflict and implements a transitional experience that will enable mankind to evolve into the full consciousness and enlightenment of the Universe, only now with the wisdom and responsibility required to remain in balance with all things. So what was deemed to be the wrath of God by many of the people of this time, was in fact just the self-regulating instinct of nature and evolution, working on all levels to allow the continued progression of evolution through humankind and the Earth.

Occasionally a more open and aware being would be able to connect with the energy of this collective transformation: a visionary, seer, prophet (although few prophets gained any real clarity as to what was happening). Tapping into the potentials of this evolutionary directive, they would translate them through the religious perceptions of their minds and thus offer their prophecies. Some of these related to the idea of a saviour coming to Earth: the 'Son of God' was to be born as man to show us the way forward and teach us what was happening within human nature.

When this idea is translated, we are left with what was indeed a gift to humanity. The 'Son of God' is in fact an entity in full communion with and with full consciousness of the Universe. This was not Jesus, the embodiment and personality of one life, but the Christ spirit, the common potential nature of all humans, exposed through the man Jesus. The intelligent Universe delivered this first exposure of the nature and enlightenment of Christ to the human race, to imprint it within our consciousness. And with this it marked a turning point in our evolution and present transition. Whether we realise this or not, that turning point has been almost indelibly imprinted within our minds and consciousness: regardless of when or by whom it was initiated, it stands commonly accepted and is used as a date reference throughout the world today. I am speaking of course of the recorded dateline of transition from BC (Before Christ) to AD (Anno Domini, "in the year of our lord").

Now before I go on to write about the exposure and affect of the nature of Christ, it makes sense for me to give my personal definition and understanding of the term. I see Christ as defining a particular level of conscious awareness that a spiritual entity can evolve, one that is potentially obtainable by all humans, and is the destined fulfilment of our present human evolution. Rather than being attributed to only one man, namely Jesus, who first exposed the full nature of Christ, it is an awareness that we all as humans are naturally evolving towards, as part of our potential human nature. The Christ is the term I would use to describe a wholly enlightened and realised spiritual entity or soul, however and wherever it may have evolved; one whose spiritual identity has been realised and now exists as the conscious energy it originated from, thus liberating its awareness to that of an eternally unique soul. Such a soul has passed through the embodiment of separate experience and evolution, to fully appreciate the cycle of creation and reunite with the conscious whole (God). At such a point, the Christ spirit exists and is directed by the needs of the conscious whole. It is inseparable from the nature of the evolving Universe and becomes, in a sense, both a servant and ambassador of that Universe.

Without this awareness, we as humans within our bodies, tend to centre our identity around the temporal personalities we create in any particular lifetime, and are driven by our instincts to maintain this personal existence and to evolve through its experiences. Eventually, through the progressive experience of many lifetimes, we come to pass through a unique transformative experience in life, one that gives us a conscious realisation as to the nature of the Universe and our soul. This is our spiritual rebirth and enlightenment, revealing the eternal nature of energy, and as our soul is energy, enlightened by its unique experience of creation, so our identity now centres around the living entity of our soul. As human beings living on the Earth we still create unique personalities, but as we exist on a level of Christ consciousness, so the personality is known to be and used as the temporary expression of the soul: the clothes that we choose to wear. From this reality we naturally begin to see and feel more as part of the collective. Our individual needs for evolution upon the Earth have been fulfilled, in that we have experienced and realised complete self-discovery. But our evolution then continues, as we learn to serve and support the collective needs of the human race, the Earth and its abundance of nature, and the Universe as a whole.

This is my personal definition and understanding of the nature of Christ, which is something we shall all find and realise through our own unique experience; it is a common point of realisation and being that unites all consciousness. Although Christ is defined and hailed as the Messiah, delivered in Jesus, what the Universe has actually delivered to us is a living example of what we are all evolving towards. This was the Universe saying to us, 'this is what you are evolving towards and becoming'. Through Christ we become Universal beings, we become the image of God: an entity of energy that is aware and intelligent, and immersed in an infinite source of potential.

If we now use this perception of Christ when looking at the man Jesus, and take away all the religious dogma and elaboration that has been built up around him over the centuries, then all we are left with is an ordinary human being, no different from me or you. Admittedly this was a human being who had reached the potential of Christ consciousness, a soul who was in the service of the Universe, and as such his life may not seem ordinary to us. But the human nature of Christ, when it is realised, is as ordinary and instinctive to that being as our present nature is to us.

Jesus' soul, in co-operation with many others at this time, was drawn to incarnate again in a conscious commitment to the Universe. It chose to come to Earth, in the same way that we all choose to incarnate, to help the collective transformation of the human race. It was not that his life was planned out or dutifully fulfilling a prophecy, for the Universe does not work in such a way, as it is always open and interactive. His commitment was to give his life completely to exposing the nature of Christ. In speaking and exposing this truth to all about him at this time in history, then due to the present balance of human nature and its sometimes destructive actions, the possible repercussions were clear.

There have been and will continue to be others who expose degrees of Christ consciousness; souls who's examples in life helps, supports and inspires our development and evolution. But the exposure of Christ through Jesus was set to mark a very definite turning point within our evolution and present transformation, and for this reason alone it stands out above nearly all others, to remain imprinted within our collective consciousness. In this respect it is not the man and personality Jesus, but the natural living example of Christ, what this can endure and achieve, that is all important to our evolution and future as a race. Jesus does not need to be held aloft and worshipped: this was an ordinary man, living by his true nature and following his heart felt instincts and commitments. What follows is, I believe, a more honest outline of what his life exposed, and how this came to serve the Universe and support our continued evolution and transition.

Firstly Jesus was conceived and born in the same manner as any human being. Mary, his mother, conceived a child through intercourse, a child that was whole in spirit: enlightened, aware of the nature of the Universe, one with God. Because of the scandal in those times, of a child conceived out of wedlock, both Mary and Joseph (Jesus' father) were afraid of what might happen to them when people found out. These fears were alleviated however by dreams and direct spiritual experiences that encouraged these two to marry and have the child, as he would have a strong impact on our future as a race.

Stories of the virgin birth are misinterpretations of the idea of the Holy Spirit, which relates to a spirit that has become fully enlightened, or 'whole'. They have been devised and used, along with other such fanatical concepts of, "the immaculate conception", as ways of purifying and deifying the images of

Mary and Jesus. There has been, and still is, much debate as to the authenticity of these concepts: basically they have been used as propaganda by the church, to disassociate Mary and Jesus from basic human nature, and to present them more as Godly beings. They are the angelic faces of the Christian Church that can sell their religion to people, and as such they could not be considered to have had sexual intercourse, something that was deemed by the fanatical religious hierarchy of the time when these ideas were first introduced, to be a dirty animal instinct (obviously they were unaware of the possible loving and spiritual nature of sex). Unfortunately this has only diminished the reality of Jesus' human nature within Christianity, and served to make Christ unreachable to us mere mortals; a useful tool for the Church, as people were told none could know Christ unless they followed Jesus, and as the leaders of the Church claimed to be the mouth pieces for Jesus on Earth, so their authority became unquestionable.

We are all free of course to portray what we choose to, just as I am doing here, but this dogma does tend to detract from the thought that, 'if Jesus was conceived and born in the same manner as any human and went on to discover and understand the nature of the Universe, to become Christ..., then why can't I do the same?' This thought, I believe, is an important part of the message the Universe was trying to deliver to the human race. As Jesus gave his life to the nature of Christ, so this became his identity above his individual personality. When he said, "I am the way", the "I" here is the nature of Christ and not that of the individual personality, Jesus. Christ is the way, the truth and the light, there for us all in our own human nature, and we do not need to follow Jesus or even believe he existed for that matter, to realise this nature.

So Jesus was as genetically human as the next man, conceived through the sexual union of man and woman, as is most common and natural to us humans. He grew up much the same as any child of that time and place in Israel: playing, learning, working, eating, sleeping. Occasionally he may have shown signs that his awareness was very open and sensitive, but basically he grew in the same manner as any one of us. Jesus was raised within the Jewish religious tradition, and so his early perceptions of God and how he related to life, were expressed according to the terms and traditions of that religion. This was the language and history he had been educated to use in this life, as tools to express his understanding of evolution and the Universe. The Jewish religion was (and still is in some places) a fairly strict and proud tradition, with a history of laws, commandments and prophets. Because of their history and their perception of the one living God, they considered themselves to be God's chosen people, and it wasn't until later in Jesus' life that he proposed all people to be equal in the eyes of God (something that in effect broke his ties with the orthodox Jewish religion and led, in part, to his execution). The message that Jesus passed on from the Universe and helped to imprint within our collective consciousness, becomes extremely clear and simple as we remove and translate the Jewish influence and terminology, it becomes Universal.

As we grow through childhood and move towards adulthood, so we begin to know and develop our own minds to a much greater depth. It is here where we begin to sense and understand our needs in this lifetime. This is our calling, our soul feeding us the curiosity, inspiration or desire, to move in the direction that offers us the best opportunity to evolve. This calling can be conscious, subtle, indirect, a revelation, absurdly coincidental, or downright mundane. The soul has many ways of creating its personality and directing its path through life. We do of course have free will and can oppose this instinct, but the only positive lesson we learn from this is that to fight the impulses and needs of our soul, is to fight and cause pain to ourselves; we come back to face the same thresholds or stumbling blocks within ourselves until we learn what we need to know to evolve beyond.

It is at this point in Jesus' life that it started to become apparent what his potential and purpose was, as regards his own soul's evolution and his service to the Universe and support of the human race. Few of us, as of yet, consciously view life from the perspective of our evolving soul. We tend to become immersed in our immediate personalities and make decisions according to the professed needs of this identity, which is just the clothing a soul chooses to wear in one particular lifetime. Those few, as in the case of Jesus, who have evolved a direct awareness of the soul, tend to have a greater clarity as to their needs and direction in life, or at least as to their next step forwards. They still have free choice, but have learned from experience to accept and embody the soul without question. It is not an acting out of destiny as such, but a case of entering into a known environment with a known will and potential. There are times when the vision of what lies ahead is crystal clear, and others when we are left to trust our hearts and have faith in our intuition. The Universe is always open and interactive so there is always room for change and innovation.

Jesus began to realise what he had come to expose to humanity: his true self, what he had evolved to become over many lifetimes, Christ. In all truth he could be or do nothing else. He was to be at the centre of this gift from the Universe to humanity, and yet he played no greater or lesser a part than anyone else involved, he just did what he could do as a human being. Jesus lived and worked as part of the community in Galilee. He had a local trade behind him through which he made his living. In fact he led such an ordinary life that the local people (later on in Jesus' life) refused to listen to what he had to say about Christ and the Universe and the potential of mankind, not on the grounds of the logic of what he had to say, but merely because they could not believe one so ordinary, who they had seen grow from a child, could ever know anything about such things, not without going through the Jewish religious order and to be authenticated.

As Jesus listened to his inner calling, so he became aware of his soul's potential in this life. Our soul is patient and persistent in its guidance, it is our true identity that carries our life in its desired direction We only need to learn to recognise and trust its calling and inspiration through heart and mind, to fully realise our potential. In reality it couldn't be more simple:

if we surrender our hearts and minds completely to our soul, then the soul can be fully embodied to guide our every step and decision, and what ever we now face in life we meet with an open heart. If the feeling is positive and we feel the flow of energy and life force through our heart, then the soul is saying, 'yes', this is a good direction..., whereas if the feeling is negative and there is no energy or motivation for something, the soul is saying, 'no', this is not something you need to experience. In the case of Jesus, before he came to speak and live the message and example the Universe wished to pass on to humanity, to mark our turning point in this evolutionary transition, his soul spent time experiencing and learning (from its own unique perspective) of the present ways and nature of the people and places around him; a kind of preparation for what was to be passed on. Such life experience was invaluable as a means of creating parables; stories that could relate the profound concepts and ideas of the Universe and of human nature, to the every day experiences of the general population.

As the time approached for the Christ nature to be fully embodied and exposed by Jesus, so the calling within him became stronger. He was pulled inside to face the possibilities of his own fears and weaknesses, the temptations that could lead to the misuse of Universal energy and awareness. This is a process we all now pass through as we evolve towards Christ. We experience an internal transition of priorities, from the selfish animal instincts (that can lead to greed, imbalance and destruction), to the selfless collective nature of Universal awareness and love.

For each of us it is a unique experience, as part of us (the fearing animal nature) faces its own death, and we alone can choose to surrender that nature and pass through its death. Through this experience our soul and spirit is reborn and embodied under new Universal directives, opening and enlightening our hearts and minds as to our true eternal identity in spirit, and establishing our unique entity within the infinite consciousness and energy of the Universe. Jesus was no different, he had to face and relinquish his desire for power and his other human frailties, before the awareness and energy of the Universe could be made freely available. If you look at this in its simplest terms it is just a natural step of evolution, removing the possible obstacles in our nature to allow a complete union between our individual consciousness and the infinite consciousness of the Universe. This makes us 'whole in spirit', and as human beings we come to exist as openings and bridges between the day-to-day life upon the ground and the energy and consciousness of the Universe.

As Jesus passed through this calling and transition, facing the potentials of his fears and desires and surrendering his life and soul to the Universe, so his spirit became whole and enlightened, and the Christ awareness was fully embodied within him. It was now free to expose the way ahead and to guide his every step through the remainder of this life, to realise the potential of marking a whole new turning point and transition within our collective evolution.

This is where the ministry really begins, where the message was etched through word and deed within our collective consciousness. Jesus became the Christ, this nature superseded his individual personality and ego and became his identity. As a completely open being, the Universe spoke and worked through him. According to the needs of the people he met with and connected with, energy could pass through him: healing, clearing, explaining, clarifying. The message to humanity was the living example of Christ, it was simple and natural:

As living souls, each of us was now to take full responsibility for our lives, thoughts and actions. We, as conscious souls, would choose our incarnations and our human potentials and circumstances. We would decide our experiences and directions, and from these learn and evolve towards our Christ nature. Christ, we were shown, was within us, it is the destined direction of our evolution upon the Earth to develop and realise this nature, and as such, it cannot be denied. We have only the free will to allow it to evolve, or to oppose it, and if we choose to oppose it then all we can learn is that this only leads to self-destructive experiences, that can then deny fulfilling the potential of our evolution at this time on Earth.

The way to develop and bring forward our Christ nature was shown to be simple, for we bring forward and expose our inner soul and feelings. It is through the experience of love that Christ comes to be realised: by laying ourselves bare, admitting and facing our fears and weaknesses, and embracing and connecting with the energy and life force of all that surrounds us. This dissolves the superficial perspectives we perceive and identify with through our ego personalities and their temporal animal natures. It breaks down the boundaries of physical separateness and substance, to bring us together in the collective and Universal identity of energy and spirit. This, we were shown, would open the doors to understanding the Universe and knowing our true eternal natures. Death would no longer be a threat or carry fear for us, and our creative potential and use of energy could abound. This is the only way, through embracing our naturally evolving Christ nature, that we can find true peace and fulfilment here on Earth.

Far from being the preaching and orders this has at times been made out to be, sent from a God full of might and wrath whose aim it is to 'teach mankind a lesson', this was a practical message of support and guidance to help the transition of the human race. While words, teachings and parables were important tools for conveying this message to humanity, here it was delivered to us and imprinted within our consciousness as a living human example and reality. Delivered through an ordinary and humble human being, that we all might know this is something we could evolve to. Of course we can romanticise about the origins, life and personality of the man who helped to expose this to us, but in reality it is just another step along the path of our evolution, and Jesus was just one lifetime of one soul that helped us along the way.

We all equally compose the human race and play our part, without which we would not have the diversity of experience that allows our unique evolution to take place here on Earth. To fight against this natural process is futile; it produces a repression of the natural flow of evolution, which in turn builds pressure, leading to destructive outbursts and destabilising our balance, both individually and thus collectively. But this is not something we can truly learn and appreciate by just being told: following the exposure of Christ and the marking of this turning point, we are left to choose the incarnations and experiences we need to learn for ourselves, which takes us into the 'time of decision' in which we now find ourselves.

And so the turning point in our transition was marked and recorded: from the Old Testament to the New Testament, from the old perceptions of and relationship with the Universe, to the new clearer ones of equality and individual responsibility. The old view of God as the lord and master, the teacher who stood above and ruled over his subjects, telling them what was right and wrong and what to do and what not to, was on its way out. This had given us monarchies, ruling dynasties, dictators, emperors, individuals given supreme power over the lives of the many who bowed to accept this rulership. God's proclaimed messengers stood above the people and dictated laws, sacrifices and rituals that had to be adhered to, to remain in God's good books, 'lest he strike you down on the spot'. This was man's view of God according to his experience of life and how his societies were governed around this time in history. Rulers could almost do as they pleased: build monuments in their own honour, kill on a whim, and make war with other nations. It all depended on their personal balance and how much such power corrupted them. The ordinary man prospered or suffered according to their rulers; God was either pleased or displeased with their actions. In a way it was an easy choice for a subject, as they did not have to take responsibility but just did as they were told, or suffered the consequences.

Then along comes Jesus (along with others around this time) who starts to speak out against this rule and says that we each of us are responsible to God for our actions, and so began the new testament or relationship with God. We were shown the potential of our natures in Christ and how to develop this to reap the rewards such awareness could bring, and we were advised of the pitfalls and weaknesses we had to face. But from this point on in history, up until the time of the 'second coming' (more of which later), we were to be left to make our own decisions and to take full responsibility for our own lives and evolution. Now we would have to speak up and form our own thoughts and relationship with the Universe. There would always be tutors and guidance available at our request (both on the spiritual planes and upon the Earth), but ultimately we were to become our own teachers as we learned to take responsibility for ourselves. It was like moving on to 'higher education', where the onus was on us to learn and we could choose how much or how little to work through in a lifetime, or even to ignore the potentials we are born with.

This transition is the only way for us to evolve as individual spiritual entities upon the Earth; the way for us to become representatives of God, the Universal intelligence; droplets within the ocean. In a sense it is a way for nature to sort the wheat from the chuff, but far from being judged by a separate God on the final day, and then rewarded or punished according to our deeds, we each of us are our own judge through a progression of lifetimes during the time of decision. Our actions and how much we learn from them is what decides how we evolve, and whether or not we are capable of coming to embody the Christ nature as our consciousness is re-opened to the Universe.

We are free to follow destructive actions, to be immersed in greed and selfishness and to ignore our conscience and karma in future incarnations; some of us even choose this way to make certain we learn. But ultimately we are only denying ourselves the potential of further evolution and enlightenment on this planet. The mental and emotional experience of following such actions always leads to pain, even if we feel extremely comfortable within our greed for a time. Pain is becoming disconnected from our soul, losing direction and purpose, and of course facing the karma and consequences of our actions, for there is nothing that we have done that passes unnoticed by the Universe and is not reflected back in our need to restore balance and evolve. In time all unbalanced and unresolved emotions and actions return to their originators, to be faced and dissolved; if we are responsible then there is nothing we can or should need to escape, as all experience has something positive to teach.

We are of course also free to choose lives that involve self-sacrifice and love, which are usually harder more demanding paths of experience. We may face losses and hardships, or be denied what we think we need to be happy, we may be cheated, walked over by the greedy, forced to sacrifice our own wants for the needs of others. Whatever the case, such a path in life requires more work and determination. We have to bring forward more of our soul and life force to succeed, and in doing so the potential to learn and evolve is much greater, thus making the transition to our Christ nature that much smoother and more easily acceptable. The choice, coming into life and throughout every decision we make, is entirely ours.

This, I believe, is an outline of the message and example Jesus helped to deliver to mankind, as regards the nature of Christ and our continued evolution. The aim for Jesus was never to establish a religion that would come to deify and worship him: one that would come to dictate 'right' and 'wrong' to others and wield the threat of condemnation, hell and damnation upon its followers. This was the doing of other people throughout our more recent history, each with their own reasons in mind. It was not unknown that this might happen, as any man that speaks out might draw followers who in turn personalise their interpretation of his words to suit their own thinking. I try to make the distinction between defining Jesus' every word and action, and exposing the part he had to play in helping our evolution through its present transition. In the end, as our nature continues to evolve, only the truth stands the test of time, while the whispers and stories that have been accumulated over the years, tend to fall by the way.

Jesus came simply to live as an example of Christ, to expose and pass on the message of what we all might become, irrelevant of creed, race, religion or colour. His life has helped and still is helping humanity in two main ways. Firstly it stands as a direct and clear exposure of the true nature of Christ. It has imprinted within our collective consciousness the potential of what our own human nature is evolving toward, offering advice and support to help this process and showing by example the miraculous realities of what Christ can create and achieve. The second way he has helped humanity, also gives us an invaluable insight to our nature. During the time he was alive, and even since that time up until the present day and beyond, he enabled us to get a clear reflection back of exactly where we stand in relation to the nature of Christ. By surrendering his personal desires and judgement upon others, to fully embody and become the Christ nature, what ever was man's reaction to him, simply reflected where they stood in relation to their own Christ nature.

Some people gave up their livelihoods, even their lives, to support this message of Christ. Some fell before Christ in fear and reverence, and where then brought to their feet to show that Christ was not above them but within them, on their level. Many were naturally uncertain as to Christ's authenticity: immersed in their day-to-day living and responsibilities, they tended to be swayed by the opinions of others who had the time to think and speak out. Rumours abounded in gossip, and rather than looking within themselves for ideas, it was much easier to believe by demanding and witnessing some miracle, or by taking somebody else's word and opinion (something we still tend to do en masse through much of our media). Finally, those who lived and worked within the religious orders of Jesus' time and place of living, especially the Jewish order, were for the most part indignant and enraged by the affront of such an ordinary man of common origins, to think he had the right to speak out about God and the Universe, especially without their permission and scholarship.

All of these reactions give us a cross-section of how different individuals and groups relate to the nature and idea of Christ. And the last of these reactions gives us an invaluable insight as to the destructive potential of the other side of our nature, that of our fearing self-preserving animal nature. It is this part of our nature that seeks power over others to try and control their thinking; something that can only be done of course, if people are willing to allow their thinking to be controlled. Such power is sought because of a person's inner fear of being exposed and being shown to be ordinary and human. The animal nature sees this as a weakness and fears it could be attacked and hurt through such exposure, even if it is only emotional pain. It can also build a privileged position in society, where its physical needs are better taken care of. So it creates whatever thought patterns it needs to convince the person not to open up and be exposed, and to consider itself above other people and higher up the food chain.

As this opening process follows the direction of our present evolution, to deny it is to repress our soul and human nature, and so the mind seeks to compensate for its fear and weakness, hence the need for a position of power. From here the internal problem is reflected out as the person tries to repress the opening and free thinking of other's consciousness, and if this fails, such fear, at its most extreme, may drive a person to destroy what ever it is that speaks out above their crafted position of power to expose their human frailties. This whole process, although greatly generalised, due to the individual nature of every person's reasoning, describes what takes place within a person who fears to face the nature and reality of Christ within themselves, to the extreme point where they feel they must deny others the opportunity.

The path of evolution towards Christ is challenging and demanding, it naturally opens us up, emotionally turning us inside out, as it dissolves the defensive instincts of our animal nature and allows our spirit to flow through, enlighten and create. This process of transformation means taking full responsibility for our souls, facing up to and learning from all of our actions, throughout all incarnations, and allowing the dominance of our animal natures to die away. Such demands from evolution can at times seem conflicting, confusing and hard to bear. As I said previously, there is nothing inherently evil or wrong with feeling our animal instincts, they are part of the foundations of our human nature and will always remain with us to some degree. Trouble only arises when we choose to ignore the progressive compulsions of our evolution, encouraging us to 'let go' of the dominance of our animal instincts, and remain with the old animal instincts out of fear (that are driven to hold on, protect the self, dominate or destroy any perceived threats, or simply run away).

The pressure created in this repression of our evolution means that the favoured animal instincts become twisted and are taken to extremes, they align to and feed our fears, internally creating thought patterns associated with the personal fears and weaknesses of the individual. These first try to justify the need to listen to our fear, and thus go on, if we allow them to, to expand into the complexities and webs that compose a distorted and disturbed mind. This will then be projected outwards in the need to dominate and twist the thinking of others and thus continue the delusions of their simple original fears. It is important to appreciate that no matter how complex or deep rooted a problem may seem to be within someone, it can always be traced back to a simple point of origin, and thus be worked through and resolved, even if it lies in the experience of a previous life. We do not need to fight our perceived or appointed enemies, simply because in the wider scheme of our soul's evolution, we can only actually be our own worst enemy, as all our actions reflect back upon us and how we evolve.

Now if we look at the Jewish elders and chief priests of Jesus' time from this perspective, it is easy to understand the reasons for their course of action. Inside they were frightened by what this man had to say. It was honest, it exposed our human nature and put us all on the same level, and it took away the illusion of the pomp and position they hid behind and left them facing themselves. Jesus was always aware of the possible reactions to what he had to say, but he chose to speak out, as to remain silent would have meant repressing his own nature and voice due to the fear of how others might react. He had committed his soul to Christ and thus surrendered any need to repress himself. And so the condemnation and falsified trial, that lead to the brutalisation and eventual crucifixion of Jesus, helped to expose to the human race just how primitive and fearful we could still be in the face of our true potential loving nature. All Jesus had done was to speak from his heart what he believed to be true, and for that, there were those among us who were willing to see him dead, simply because they were too frightened to face themselves and allow others the freedom of speech.

Strangely enough, on a parallel with this, even today there are those in the Christian church, and amongst many other religions, within their rankings and hierarchies, who, if they were faced with someone willing to speak out in a similar manner to Jesus, denying the self proclaimed authority of their religion, might seek to destroy him in some way. Obviously their methods might not be so blatantly brutal (although people are still tortured and killed in some countries for speaking their religious or political beliefs). The more fanatical followers of the Christian church or other such mass religions, usually employ finger pointing and condemnation, sometimes to an obsessive degree. While these attitudes remain merely as remnants of old, out dated modes of thinking, perpetuated by fearful closed minds, the power structures and struggles still exist and still serve to expose our primitive nature. When the priority in a religion moves away from discovering, understanding and sharing your own unique soul, to dictating and controlling the thinking and actions of its followers, then it can become so choked in fear and anger that people are willing to go to war and kill one another over differences of words and ideas.

Once again there are many such examples within our history, even within the present day, that expose the hard ways we are learning our lessons. And as for those high in the ranks of religion or government in our present day: a truly good man does good deeds because it is the natural instinct and the expression of his soul, not because he seeks some promised reward, or praise, or followers, or because he is told to do so by his Church or the writings in the Bible. We cannot kid the Universe into believing we are holy or enlightened, we can only become these things naturally by opening ourselves up to the Universe. We all have to face up to and work through the destructive tendencies of our nature, they cannot be bypassed; only when we accept them and embrace them do we begin to have control over them, and from here we have the ability to surrender them.

It was the example of Jesus in the face of anger, hatred, condemnation, brutalisation, and eventual crucifixion, that really helped to imprint the message and nature of Christ within our collective consciousness. Jesus remained true to his soul and beliefs regardless of the accusations and threats, and as he no longer listened to his own fears, so he helped to expose the fears of others and how they had developed. He understood why fear and anger was sometimes brought forward in others. By standing openly before them he gave them a reflection and experience of how they were repressing and treating their own soul's potential: the more anger they directed at him, then the more they exposed how fearful and repressed they were inside.

Eventually Jesus was handed over to the Romans and crucified, due to the insistence of the Jewish elders and chief priests, but he offered no defence when arrested and remained true to his beliefs at the expense of his life. This helped to indelibly imprint the nature of Christ within us: he showed by example that allegiance to the soul and its freedom of expression, was to be valued above the physical experience of one lifetime. The body we are born into in any one lifetime, and come to grow, experience and evolve through, may pass away or be taken from us in many ways. But the words of truth, the energy and enlightened nature of our souls, are things that cannot be taken away by another: they will always have been, and live on eternally as part of our unique evolution, imprinted within our collective experience.

And so we come to the final example that Jesus delivered to us, the example that helped to inspire those close to him, who feared for their own lives after his crucifixion, so that they could go on to record and spread the word and example of Christ, regardless of the risks they now knew to be involved. I am speaking of course of the resurrection. I do not believe that Jesus chose to return to his physical body, and that the resurrection was in fact his soul re-entering the body and raising it from the dead. A soul re-entering the body long after it seemed dead is no new miracle. There was the raising of Lazarus and the widower's son at Nain according to the Christian Bible, and throughout history right up to the present day there have been documented cases of people clinically 'dying' and then coming back to life some time later.

On occasions a soul chooses to re-enter the body after having disincarnated (if the opportunity arises and as long as the body is capable of being revived), simply because there is the potential to learn and achieve more during that lifetime. It takes a lot of time and energy to grow through childhood and establish a personality that is capable of continuing the soul's evolution. The human body itself is an astonishing example of the precise and painstaking creative work of evolution, and it is rare that one is allowed to go to waste if a soul still has the potential to live through it. The human race had little need to be shown that the body could come back from what seemed like the dead. This could be explained in many other ways, as people might say that Jesus was never dead in the first place. There have been, and still are today, many conspiracy theories about the death and resurrection of Jesus. To come back into the physical body offers almost no insight as to what lies beyond our physical incarnations, and it is my understanding that the true resurrection of Jesus had this purpose in mind and looked to define the idea of 'eternal life'.

After Jesus had disincarnated, and his body had been sealed away in its tomb, it was then that his entity, supported by other enlightened souls, began to dematerialise his body through the manipulation of energy. The aim of this was to remove all trace of his physical body, to show that it is something we do not need to hold on to, and to deny it being used by others to propagate their cause. This then enabled his spiritual entity and awareness to re-manifest itself into its previously recognisable form, and therefore show that the soul cannot be destroyed by any amount of physical pain or death. It continues to evolve and live on eternally in its true form, that of a unique conscious entity of energy.

The genetics of a human is only one of the possible forms our entity can choose to enter and evolve through. The physical body of one lifetime, the thing through which you presently live and breath and read these words, is something we may become very attached to (every one of them is unique), but it is merely the vehicle our soul uses to grow into, move around and interact, and eventually pass out of, the human experience of life on Earth. Our body is the form our soul chooses to use along its path of evolution and enlightenment.

With this in mind, Jesus looked to re-manifest his soul into the form that those close to him would recognise, to show that the pain of his death was past and had taken nothing. While he was no longer with them in the flesh, he was as alive as he had ever been, and would always be with them to support them in the work that lay ahead. This is the reality of 'eternal life' and of the 'resurrection': it is not that we come back into a physical body to live through it for all eternity, as the limitations of life on Earth would start to become tedious after a while and the soul would feel trapped. The resurrection represents the soul's own personal conscious awakening to all the lives it has led, and the integration of these into one whole being. As we experience this realisation in conscious life, so we truly realise our eternal nature, and this then supersedes the physical body and personality as our central identity. The perspective we gain from this new identity exposes our place within an infinite

Universe, and the energy that is our conscious entity now fully realises its eternal nature in the 'real' experience of life, and so can never truly die again.

After this realisation, birth and death are no longer barriers or cold and fearful cut off points, they are now the conscious gateways we can choose to pass through. So the 'resurrection' is our own personal awakening to the lives we have led and the personalities we have been, all of which have helped to walk the path towards our full enlightenment, and now compose the unique nature of our enlightened souls. This true resurrection leads us to a time when our souls can freely manifest upon the Earth (or elsewhere), without the need to pass through the tunnel of physical genetics, unless this is so desired. Of course we will not have the same physical experience of embodiment in life, but then we will no longer experience its limitations either.

When compared with our present conscious day-to-day reality, some of this may sound a little far fetched and seem to belong on the shelves of science fiction. But in reality it is as ordinary and as natural a progression as say, the evolution of primates to humans. When we consciously evolve to a level of Christ consciousness and awareness, we become the intelligent and conscious Universe (or God). The awareness and nature of the Universe lives and breathes through us, it becomes our sight and perception, and the doors to its infinite potential are open to us. In the spirit, without form, we can manifest or dematerialise energy, we can choose to incarnate and experience any particular star system or planet. The whole process and direction of our evolution works according to need and attraction: where there is a need for light, energy or stimulated evolution, then souls are drawn in to incarnate or to support from the spiritual levels. In the case of the Earth, many souls are committed to this process of transformation, Jesus being only one. The things that we choose to call miracles, simply because such control of energy is not common to our day-to-day reality and perception of life, were, from the Universal perspective of Christ, just the natural mediumship and productive use of the ever present latent energy of the Universe, according to need and attraction.

If we look at this in its simplest reality, then Jesus was a complete embodiment of our Christ nature, an open and evolved spiritual entity born into and living as a human being. His personal and individual needs, the things that dictated his direction and focus in life, became the collective needs of the human race, and more directly, the needs of the every day people around him. He felt their loss and pain, their blocks and negative karma, not because he felt it was his duty to do so, or because he felt charitable, but because it is natural for the completely open sensitivity of Christ to feel the nature of all you are connected to. Jesus therefore felt drawn in by the needs of those around him, this was a self-regulating need to be balanced and whole again.

Healing is not a case of just forgiving sins at will; it took place at this time when another soul opened itself up before Jesus. By recognising their need and through the humility of asking forgiveness, so the two could connect, and the energy needed to dissolve the dark aura and restore the balance could flow through, thus healing whatever the affliction was (physical, mental, emotional). It is just the same as a current of energy balancing itself out, according to where it is drawn. Jesus had to have an external need to complete the circuit, to allow energy to flow through, to heal or re-manifest limbs. This is a natural part of the potential nature of Christ, the ability to allow energy to pass through and to manifest or dematerialise matter according to need and attraction.

Rather than Jesus being the miracle worker, it is Christ that allows us to be the medium for the creative energy of the Universe, for this intelligent source is as responsible for our healing as it is for our existence in the first place. The message from the Universe is not to hold our image of Jesus aloft in awe, and to bow before a greatness that is way beyond the reach of us mere mortals. The message is to respect that what there was to admire in Jesus is also within us, and that by taking full responsibility for our lives and actions, and following the strongest instincts of our own heart and soul, we too evolve towards and can become Christ. Of course you personally don't have to call it Christ, its name is irrelevant, it is just human nature. You do not have to believe in Christ, Jesus, miracles, or anything I have written in this whole book. The truth that you really need, the only truth that can lay your fears and questions to rest, lies within you, and comes only from the experience of yourself.

Jesus has always been singled out as the front man when it comes to the exposure and imprinting of Christ within our collective consciousness. In many cases to the extreme of being worshipped, not just in Christianity, but also by many cults and other religions. As the intensity of focus is nearly always directed upon Jesus, so it is easy to neglect the work and sacrifices of other souls. All the people of this time played a part in how Christ was exposed to the human race: the disciples, those who allowed themselves to be healed, the chief priests and Jewish elders, the Romans, the crowds that watched what was taking place. All of these helped to give a reflection of the nature of Christ and to imprint it within our collective mind. In some ways Jesus part was the easiest to live out: his soul was completely committed to exposing Christ and allowed the Universal will to direct his every move through life. At times he could see ahead so clearly he knew exactly what was to happen next, and offering no resistance he allowed it to be.

It was the disciples however, who after Jesus' death did the work of sharing the message and example of Christ with many other peoples around the world, and thus brought Christ to the forefront of our consciousness. The disciples exposed to us a much more recognisable human reaction to the nature of Christ: through their relationships with Jesus and among themselves they reflect back the doubts and fears we may come to face as the nature of Christ is brought forward and exposed within us; doubts and fears that are still common to the human race today...: Who was this person Jesus? Where did he come from? Was he human? Why did he speak about Christ, deliverance, and the second coming? Were the things he did real or trickery? What does he want from me? People will surely think I am mad if I talk about him? What will people think of me if I talk about Christ, or share my deepest fears and hopes? How will they react? These are just a few of the doubts and questions that come to mind, and despite all of these, some of the disciples went on to write about, talk of, and even heal in the name of Christ, at the cost of their own lives.

In my opinion the disciples had a much harder part to play in the exposure of Christ. They did not have the certainty of Jesus: some left their livelihoods and families, they made mistakes, misunderstood things and argued amongst themselves at times. Take Judas Iscariot as an example: his name has had to bare the brunt of many people's scorn throughout the centuries for being the one who was said to of betrayed Jesus, and yet his own thinking and reasoning may have been a simple mistake:

Judas had previously been associated with the Zealots before he came to work with Jesus, a sometimes violent revolutionary group who saw the occupying Romans as the main oppressor to the freedom of the Jewish nation. Jesus was someone who spoke out against authority and promised revolutionary change, which was possibly one of the reasons why Judas was first drawn to him. After spending time with Jesus, I believe Judas was left in no doubt as to the ultimate power of Christ, but he was impatient for revolution and change. Judas's so called betrayal of Jesus may of originated from the thinking that if the authorities confronted Jesus and arrested him, this would force his hand and he would have to use the power at his disposal to destroy the Romans and thus leave Israel free.

I am not saying this is exactly what happened, this is just one possibility. But it demonstrates how easy it is to follow faulty logic; to act for what you feel would be the best outcome, only to see everything go in a completely different direction, one that Judas felt he could not live with. Of course his reasoning may of just been that he needed the money, and he believed that Jesus would come to no ultimate harm, either way, as humans, it is easy to make mistakes. Without Judas's actions Jesus may never have left the immense impression that he did, hence Judas played his part like everyone else, and his condemnation serves no positive good to anyone; it shows how quick we can be to point the finger away from ourselves.

Despite all of this, it was the disciples, having to face and carry the hardships of their human weaknesses and fears, who freely decided to spread the word and example of Christ. A decision based upon their own personal experience of Jesus and his Christ nature, and ultimately based upon their own personal experiences and beliefs. They are the ones who give us the clearest comparison between our present nature and the potential of Christ. They did much of the hard work in helping to pass on and imprint the nature of Christ within our collective consciousness, and in firmly marking the turning point in our collective evolution.

Since this time there have been many examples of the nature of Christ. Jesus and his disciples certainly do not hold the monopoly on Christ, they merely mark one of the openings through which it now comes to enter us all. There have been many others who have come to expose Christ in the way of their own unique soul. There are and have been many unsung heroes and sacrifices that pass unnoticed by the collective majority. Rest assured however, all of these experiences help to guide and support the collective human race towards realising the true nature of Christ within themselves. And look upon this time, if only for a moment, not as Jesus commanding us to live a certain way, but merely as the Universe gifting us a sight, of where the destiny of our evolution is taking us.

I have written about this whole period, relating to the first exposure of Christ and to the turning point in our evolution, according to the personal discoveries I made within myself. Simply by spending time immersed in my own heart and mind and through my own connections with the collective mind. My search in life was internal: for answers, for truth, for some driving force or purpose behind being human in this day-to-day existence. My search was unconditional: I had not previously considered many of the things I have written about here, and I had no affiliations with any of our present world religions and knew very little about them. I ask you to look at Jesus here, not as a Christian or through the eyes of any religion, but simply as an ordinary human being, no different from you.

All of what came forward in me, came from a completely open and free mind; the discoveries felt pure and untainted, they were exposed as surprises and revelations that seemed to come forward of their own free will. Nothing that I felt a need to know and understand was withheld, even the experiences of previous lives were exposed according to their connection with this present life (something I certainly had not considered or looked into previously), and they came forward in such a way as to integrate with this present life and to leave no doubt in my mind. Such personal experiences I do appreciate may mean little to anyone else, but they are the things that have carried me to my present understanding of the Universe, and to the words that have composed this manuscript.

I certainly do not ask you to take my word for these things, for I know that it is part of human nature for the soul to need to find its own answers. Whether from your own experience you have a belief in or understanding of Christ and the lives of Jesus and his disciples, is not the issue here. Even if you feel they never even existed and that Christ is just another ancient myth, they still offer deep insights into human nature and to how we are evolving. What I feel is important about this time, and what I have tried to convey here, is the conscious turning point in our evolution that was marked by the exposure of our Christ nature. Whether we believe in this or not, without having made its impact, then I would not be here to discuss this and you would not be reading.

To me, from my experience, Christ represents our own personal discovery and awakening to our true identity within the Universe. It is a unique experience of the soul, and as such, it is something no science can ever measure or prove, and no religion can ever posses and deliver to you. Only we can realise and experience it for ourselves. Before such an experience of self-discovery, there will always be doubts and room for speculation. I would urge everyone that reads this to accept nothing and to question everything; only your own discoveries will free you of doubt and lead you to become certain. We can choose to clothe God in whatever language, culture, or science our upbringing conditions us to, or our state and structure of mind aligns to: the extreme of a cult..., the comfort and romanticism of a mass established religion..., the hard and straight facts of science..., the atheism of a lack of interest or care..., or simply the unique and free expression of our soul, living life freely from day-to-day.

The Time Of Decision

It is from the exposure of Christ and of mans' many different reactions to this Christ nature, that a clear definition of 'good' and 'bad' are established, the light and dark sides of human nature. From the time of this turning point up until the present day, we have been learning to take individual responsibility for our soul's evolution, and thus help to support and direct the collective experience of the human race. This has been the essential focus of our evolution since the exposure of Christ; it is the time of decision, where souls freely choose their experiences and direction, according to their needs to evolve. We prepare our incarnations and have to take responsibility for our decisions and actions throughout each lifetime, hopefully learning and evolving towards the awareness gained in Christ. There is no need for people to be forcefully subjected to laws or religious judgements, there is no real judge as to 'right' and 'wrong' apart from our individual soul in accordance with its needs to learn. It serves no purpose for someone to be told what is wrong and forced not to consider it for themselves.

The whole aim of this process of evolution is to allow humankind the experience of both light and dark sides: to recognise, accept and know the two for what they are and where they lead, and from this experience to decide the soul's direction forward. Some souls have already made a committed choice to 'light', to follow their heart felt instincts and soul intuition, and to evolve towards the enlightenment of Christ throughout their chosen incarnations. This is certainly not an easy path, as with this being a time of transition the collective mind is often confused and chaotic, making it difficult for a soul to remain open and balanced. Other souls may need to experience more of their dark side and the pain and destructiveness this can lead to, before they can see it for what it is and learn to let go of its dominance.

Individually we face the conflict within our own nature, whether we recognise it or not, but collectively we are supporting each other, and it is here where social structures and systems of government are formed. The destructive or negative actions of one soul, can help to expose the dark side of our nature to a wider scope of people, which in turn can lead to a positive reaction and help to bring forward a collective response that advances and teaches the individuals involved. There is no ultimate evil: all experiences, even the most destructive and depraved, lead us to a greater understanding of our nature and its evolution. The dark side has no real independent power, only the illusions our fears are allowed to create, and the destructive actions this can sometimes lead to. Ultimately the only progressive power is the light: this is the positive energy and driving force to all evolution, and it needs the dark only as a void to fill to maintain the structured balance of time and space, and as a comparison to expose the light. In this respect the two are completely interdependent: there is no light without darkness and no darkness without light. An extreme of light is inspirational and creative, while an extreme of darkness is fearful and destructive. Light composes and expands life, while darkness frames and engulfs it, and because of this, we as humans have formed the concepts of good and evil, that relate to the light and dark sides of our nature.

If you were to take a close look at any of the cultures, societies, religions and tribes, that have risen and fallen throughout this whole period of transition, then you would find traces of this battle between the light and dark sides of human nature, between 'good' and 'evil'. This idea is everywhere: in myths and legends, stories and fairy tales, religion, even science to a degree questions the light and dark natures of matter. Whether we have been aware of it or not, the basic themes and direction of our evolution have been staring us in the face for centuries.

Evil is usually depicted as being manipulative and cunning, greedy and self-interested, power hungry, violent, fearful and destructive, the embodiment of all that is seen to be bad in human nature. While good on the other hand, is portrayed as being brave and courageous, honest and truthful, giving, loving and self-sacrificing. These are the light and dark aspects of human nature, they represent the open and loving spiritual instinct to embrace life and evolve, and the extreme and fearful animal instinct of self-preservation above all other life. Evil is shown to be motivated by fear, and in our stories it is usually shown to be seeking to destroy good, to achieve power, and to manipulate people and the world according to its greedy desires for more. Good on the other hand is shown to stand up to evil regardless of the threats. It may be hurt, humiliated, even killed, but ultimately it is shown to be the stronger and keeps coming back to eventually win over evil. This is the simple message behind many of the myths, legends, folk laws and religions that have been passed around throughout this time of decision we now find ourselves in. Even today most of the underlying plots to our films and forms of entertainment are based upon this common theme. It is etched within our collective mind, surfacing again and again throughout the ages, in different guises and forms, and we continue to watch and enjoy it again and again, although not always realising its deeper connotations.

This time of decision has dominated the last two thousand years of our history, from the exposure of Christ up to the present day. Basically, for this whole period of time, the human race has been left to its own devices. It is an experimental time: our future potential has been exposed in the nature of Christ, and now we are left to face, expose and in a sense exorcise the dark and destructive side of our human nature, through the experiences of many incarnations, as many as each individual soul requires up until the second coming. This whole period can de divided into three main progressive stages of transformation, relating to the breakdown and removal of the dominance of our old animal instincts and directives, to prepare the way for the new spiritual directives of Christ:

The first stage is where souls first begin to take more responsibility for themselves, and where the potentials of their dark sides are brought forward from within them. The old forms of government, those with single god like rulers commanding many subjects and followers, such as imperialism and sovereign states, are continually broken down as more people speak out and seek independence. Empires and rulerships are built up and brought down again with little long-term stability, as the human race collectively searches for a system of government that offers more individual freedom and equality. Sadly any attempt to establish a fair government of equality, eventually meets its fate at the hands of those who seek to dominate and conquer.

Along side this, the Christian church begins to spread and build a following, with the basic message of Christ being made available to the masses. Here again though positions of power are established over peoples lives, and hence the dark side of human nature is drawn in as the church begins to wield its dictatorial and sometimes merciless destructive power. The word Christ can be used by anyone to front anything they choose, but individuals will always be responsible for their actions, and throughout history it is the actions of the people that speak of their true motivation. Hence there have been numerous atrocities carried out over the centuries in the name of Christianity. Other Christ like religions grew around this time (for example Buddhism, established several hundred years B.C..., and Islam, beginning several hundred years AD). Although on paper their ideas and rituals may have seemed to differ greatly, the essential message was of change and enlightenment for the human soul; that we might all become enlightened as to our true spiritual nature.

The second stage takes us from the dark ages of fear and disorder (around 500A.D.), through the Middle Ages of new migrations and invasions (beginning in the 10th century), and on towards the renaissance of the 14th century. This is where the dark side of human nature is brought more to the surface and out into the open. There is very little stability in this time: people struggle for power, rulers rise and fall in quick succession, feudalism begins to dominate as there is little central or collective government. There is a great deal of gloom over the majority of the people of this time: the battle between good and evil, whilst having its field within our individual souls, became much more externalised. The dark side of human nature was beginning to take a hold on the human systems of government. Greed and the all-conquering attitude dominated, while prophecies of doom abounded and knowledge and freethinking became a crime in itself in some places (often punished by death).

Nearing the end of this stage and the beginning of the final stage (although they greatly overlap and there are no clear dividing lines), the plague of the 14th century, called the 'black death', wiped out millions of people across the world (Europe and Asia), killing more of the worlds population than any other disease or war in our history to date. This again summed up the human experience of this time, dark and fearful, as the dark side of human nature was brought out into the open and people were confused about their direction and their relationship to God. This was of course something that needed to happen for the dark side of our nature to be experienced and eventually exorcised, so essentially this is positive progress, although the picture painted by history may seem the opposite on occasions.

The final stage brings us up to the present day. It begins around the time of the renaissance in Europe, where the importance of the individual, freethinking and creativity were brought forward as the primary focus of human nature within society. This led onto new explorations, colonisation, increased world trade and communications, the rise of scientific thinking, the industrial revolution, the French revolution, the American revolution, the gradual independence of colonies. The old systems of sovereign rulership were gradually being replaced with new collective forms of government, although at times it was a long, bloody and hard fought process. The term renaissance literally means, 'rebirth', and human beings began to appreciate and believe in their potential once again, to exist as part of a collective race and to follow their own individual path of evolution and achieve greater enlightenment and awareness. This reflected in the re-opening of the human mind: old spiritual philosophies originating from the early stages of this process of transformation, when we were more intuitively spiritually aware, were revived and progressed. New scientific thinking and discoveries also came forward, new creativity in art, music and literature. Nothing seemed impossible, and what was laughed at or condemned in one century, was then proved to be true and commonly accepted in the next.

Along side this gradual flight of the human soul, the darker side of human nature still resisted change and fought to hold back new thinking, often through the guise of the church. Now that it was more exposed, it slowly adapted to become more accepted within the institutions of the Church and the developing governments, in a way that was no longer so brutal and blatant, but far more deceptive and manipulative. Positions of power were sought, for this was where ideas could be propagated and thus thinking controlled. Two main political ideals for the government of societies were gradually developed, those of communism and democracy, and these lead us up to the present day. The only thing that denies them being realised in their idealistic and natural forms, is the persistent greed of the dark side of human nature.

Communism and democracy are certainly not as dissimilar as they have been made out to be in recent times: both support the common theme of the rights and equality of the individual, and in this respect they underline the whole purpose of this time of decision, namely for the soul to accept individual responsibility for its evolution, and create the space and freedom to decide upon its path into the future. Communism is based upon the collective responsibility and use of resources, with people's creativity and labour being directed towards the common good; it is not something that can be enforced and governed as such, as the spirit of co-operative communities will come to be realised naturally as we move beyond our primitive greed and evolve to appreciate a more collective awareness, and to use resources responsibly. Democracy is based upon social equality and respect for the individual, and is about the informed choice of government, by the people, for the people.

Again, as of yet, it has not been able to be realised in its true form, due to the inequalities and deceit created by human greed. Slowly we are learning our lessons. The priorities of these two systems of government are clearly the same however, and I believe that it will be a merging and combination of these two ideals that will naturally come to form the foundations of our future world governments, as the dominance of human greed is superseded by our Christ nature.

For the most part, across the globe, we have reached a point whereby each soul has become individually responsible for itself. Remnants of old outdated religious thinking and dictatorships still battle it out, and some peoples still struggle for their independence and freedom of thought and speech, but the collective balance has shifted towards individual freedom, and continues to gather momentum. The greedy and self-destructive nature of human beings is undeniably exposed to us all, in our destructive and ignorant industrial commercialism and the competitive world economies that seem to have become central to our systems of government; valuing individual wealth to be the measure of achievement in life. As our collective mind is re-opened and our potential nature in Christ is exposed once more, then we as individuals are forced to examine ourselves and to decide our future. This of course is swayed by the balance of how we have lived our lives and evolved throughout this time of decision. There is no external judge: either our soul is capable and ready to embrace the Universal nature and awareness of Christ..., or, it needs to move on to experience other incarnations and continue its preparatory evolution elsewhere.

I have purposely skipped over the fine details of the last two thousand years of history, the mass of names, dates, events and places, for the simple reason that it is easy to get lost within them and thus miss the overview of evolution's priority through this time. Individually, on a soul level, this has given us individual responsibility and the potential to become aware of our Universal nature. Collectively this has then been reflected in the gradual breakdown of old dictatorial systems of government, and the gradual development and establishment of new, more collectively governed ones. While it is a continual and on-going process of transformation, the subtle divisions of these three stages, helps to describe how the dominance of our self-preserving animal nature (the source of the dark and destructive side of human nature) is being evolved out and replaced. First it is contacted deep within ourselves and afforded the opportunity to be expressed..., gradually it is brought more collectively out into the open, where it can be faced and exposed for what it is..., and finally it is fully exposed within our societies, economies and systems of government (in a world that would rather destroy itself than give up the compulsion towards commercialism and greed), so that we can experience and appreciate its destructive repercussions, and thus choose to move beyond its primitive nature. Regardless of the theory involved, it is only the very real experience of the dark sides of our nature, over the last two thousand years, that will certify the lessons of responsibility and balance we have needed to learn. This time of decision is what has enabled us to become so diverse and individual; something that will help to open the door to new thinking and creation within the Universe.

Upon the ground it has been a long, sometimes chaotic and hard fought process of change and transition. All the fearful and negative thought patterns that needed to be challenged and removed from our collective mind, had to be exposed and worked through in such a way so as not to make life too intense and burdensome. Suicide has become a more common occurrence today, simply because at times, it is easy for a soul to become so immersed in the daily struggle of life that the light of hope and purpose fades to nothing. Just ask yourself what true purpose do our modern societies advocate? The fact that some people choose to take their own lives, says a lot about the kind of world we live in. And yet the more we have invested of ourselves in this time, the more we have chosen to face and work through, then the more joy we shall experience as this transition is made complete. To know and feel the Universe running through your veins is an indescribable emotion that nothing can compare with: "where once was the trickle of a stream, now a mighty river flows..."

Throughout this time of decision, concepts of Heaven and Hell have been created and developed, illustrated and propagated by different religions and peoples. Many of these have been literalised, and thus have been taken literally by future generations. For the most part, the ideals of Christ have been personified in the characters of Jesus and the Buddha (to name a few examples), while the dark side of our nature has been personified in the character of Lucifer, the Devil or Satan (which means, 'adversary' or 'oppose'), a purely evil being who controls many minions and demons, each relating to a particular weakness or destructive tendency in human nature, stemming from our selfish animal instincts. Over the years, visions of heaven and hell have been used by religious leaders to convert people to their controlled way of thinking and to keep them in line once there. In truth though they are merely metaphors, often presented to the extreme to induce hope or fear as a means of controlling and dictating peoples thoughts and actions.

Christ, Satan, demons, are just metaphorical characters used to tell the story of the human predicament. They have no real existence outside of ourselves and are never independent of human nature. We are composed of the two sides and potentials, and we alone give life to these principles. Christ is just a conceptual level of awareness, only a potential, until it is born as a reality through our own unique experience; only then is it brought to life through our union and self-realisation. Similarly, Satan and demons are just concepts of potentially destructive actions. A person can wilfully draw forward and act upon destructive energy, making real the possibilities (demons) of deceit, greed, violence, murder, rape, and so on, but ultimately they alone are responsible. To say someone has a 'demon' within them, just personifies the act itself, and this has been used at times to remove human responsibility. The demon is just an imaginary construction of the fear that led the person to committing the act in the first place, after which their soul's way ahead is distorted, at least until they recognise and work to overcome the fear (thus facing and destroying their demons). Metaphors such as Satan and demons have no independent existence or reality; they have no real power to be able to deny our continued evolution, they merely serve as characterised tools (although now outdated for most of us), to help to expose the potentially destructive side of our fearing animal nature, and thus compel us towards our true enlightened spiritual nature.

Ultimately there are no such places as heaven or hell, where souls go to reside after death. There is no literal place we physically enter where God and angels reside for eternity, nor any place of fire and demons where the soul is eternally damned. This period of transition is just a temporary experience of our soul's evolution, a natural progression, carrying the Earth's evolution forwards and opening its experience up to the rest of the Universe. Heaven and hell reflect different human perspectives and states of mind, they describe our different emotional and spiritual perceptions of what lies beyond death.

Heaven represents the 'heavens', the above and beyond of the rest of the Universe and its infinite intelligence and resources. Entering heaven, means entering the consciousness of eternity, rediscovering our soul identity and Universal awareness. It is a state we pass in and out of between incarnations, but one that is born eternal as we consciously surrender our animal natures and become the Christ. Hell on the other hand, is a temporary state and perception. It reflects the pain of realisation a soul that passes out of life may experience. Having led a fairly dark and greedy or destructive existence, it is faced with the reality of its positive needs and the potential that has not been fulfilled. From here the soul is encouraged to take responsibility for what it may have ignored in life, to face and work through the same weaknesses in the future incarnations. Ultimately we create our own expectations of what we first come to experience after death. The bindings of our imaginations are the first things we come to experience and thus have to pass through to unite with our whole consciousness and reacquaint ourselves with the truth.

Hell is like living a whole lifetime ignoring the challenges of your inner needs to evolve and living for selfish reasons and pleasures. It may be the kind of modern life people look at and say, "they have plenty of money, and don't seem to care about others..., they treat people badly and just seem to get away with it... Where is the justice in that..? How can there be a God..?" In reality though there is no getting away with anything: a life spent seeking selfish pleasures above the needs of the soul (for there is nothing wrong with pleasure in itself of course), or committing crimes against others, directly or indirectly, leaves the person fairly dark and empty inside (although it is a lesson some souls need to experience for a time to learn). Imagine how you would feel having lived a whole lifetime following greed and chasing wealth, believing this to be the ultimate aim, only to have to face the repercussions of all your negative actions after death, and to see life in its true soul perspective and realise the potential you have passed by. There is no getting away with anything, as every experience needs to be faced up to enable us to learn and grow. All we really do through extreme selfish and destructive actions is deny our own soul further evolution and enlightenment, the only truly sustainable pleasure.

Through this whole age of transition, religions, cults, even science, have created ways of conceptualising our human nature and its relationship with the Universe. They all have their own history, perspectives and languages, justifying the basis for belief: be it prophecy, the example of a highly evolved human being, or the common tangible experiences of our five measurable senses. They have all in their way helped humans to evolve, to see and understand their nature and to come together and support each other. But where they all tend to fall down, as a result of people closing their minds to new and shared thinking, is when they try to dictate human thought and behaviour: to define the 'right' and 'wrong' for us all. It is here where they try to take responsibility away from the individual and deny them the experience of finding their own certain answers, and this in itself opposes the directives of our present evolution. No amount of people, no matter how strong their beliefs give the impression of being, can stand against this tide of our transition and deny its progression, for this is what has created and carried our every step in evolution.

It is not religion or science that is responsible for manipulating thinking, but the individuals that have acted in their name. Every external action reflects an internal thought or feeling, as there is a reason for everything. Those that look to dictate to and condemn or punish others for their non-conformist beliefs, merely reflect the internal repression and fear they have of their own free thinking natures. While those that hide within a religion and behind the beliefs of others, expose the internal fear of having to take responsibility for ourselves: a priest can bless, forgive, or condemn you…, a scholar can praise or deny your work…, and you can hide behind their decision and try to make the best of day-to-day life if you so choose.

Of course there are many people who successfully use the framework of a religion or a particular school of thought to further and express their understanding of the Universe. But this is because they are not judgmental and retain an open mind. As soon as the mind closes, then nothing new can pass through and thinking becomes distorted. Over the centuries there have been numerous atrocities committed in the names of God, Allah, Christ and Jesus, and in the name of scientific advancement. But it will always be the individual perpetrators of such destructive actions who are responsible. They will have to face their own conscience and karma. They will have to learn to evolve, just as we can learn from what we have seen and experienced from them.

Anyone can commit a crime, claim to prophesy or speak for God, and they can choose to do it in who's ever name they wish. I can kill in the name of Jesus, claiming the people I kill are evil or primitives..., or I can wipe out an entire population at the push of a button that I have decided are my enemies, thanks to the scientific knowledge at my disposal. Whatever the case, I alone am responsible for how I direct my actions.

Throughout this whole time of transition and still within the present, there have been and still are, many people and groups of people who believe themselves to be special, chosen, or privileged in some way, as regards their social status or their beliefs in God and the Universe: be they Jews, Muslims, Christians, Jehovah's witnesses and members of minority cults, leaders, politicians, celebrities or just arrogant scientific scholars (to name a few). And yet one of the things I am most certain of and would like to pass on through this book, is, that as human beings, there are no special or chosen people. We are of course free to believe we are superior to others, because we live or think in a certain way that others choose not to, or we currently posses huge sums of the worlds resources. But in the eyes of God, the eyes of the Universe, of creation, of evolution...., there are only individual souls. We are judged by ourselves in relation to our potential to evolve, and by the lives that we lead as human beings. We all lead different lives, we discover and express ourselves in different ways, we reach different levels of awareness within the Universe, but by our nature and potential, we are truly all equal, and exist as an inseparable part of the collective that is God.

The Second Coming

Writing about the 'Second Coming' is entering into what might be deemed as prophecy. Indeed there are numerous prophecies dedicated to exposing this idea, some of which reveal a degree of truth as to our direction, once the religious language is translated and the dogma removed. From my personal experience, I have found that when you allow your conscious awareness to withdraw from its immediate Earthly thoughts and day-to-day perceptions, from the on-going and intricate demands and relationships of the personality, so it is released and able to gain an overview of the human race, the Earth, evolution and the Universe (depending on your focus and thought guidance). The further you drift, the greater your overview, and the more collective your perspective of life becomes. As the dominance of the temporal physical world subsides, so the structure of its dimensions begin to disintegrate and time-scales no longer apply. You begin to experience and know things by embracing (even becoming) its wholistic energy, which encompasses everything, from physical form to the spiritual potential and directives. As you return to your physical being and personality, so these experiences can be translated and thus related, according to the openness of your own mind and the available diction and perceptions of the time in which you live. An open mind is a two-way window through which our awareness can take flight and discover the Universe, and also through which the Universe can enter our minds to reveal its nature and purpose, and to speak through us.

My own drifting journeys of awareness stemmed from an inner need I did not really understand at the time; 'letting go' is the only way I can explain the feeling and impulse. I let go of all that had been put upon me in life, through absorption and education, to discover what was left, what was true, heartfelt and real. From there my awareness seemed to direct itself, and without preconceptions it gradually revealed the things I have now come to write. I have felt and experienced this whole transition and the nature of the Second Coming of Christ, and I appreciate that how I have returned to translate these experiences will always be personal to my sight and perception of life. I feel the term 'Second Coming' is misleading, in that the nature of Christ has always been with us in our own potential natures. This time is more an awakening of Christ than it is a second coming. I uphold that nothing is written until it is experienced as a physical reality and made real. We all have the ability to act and react within the moment. But the general direction of our evolution and the transformation it is presently carrying us through, has certain definite aims and directives, and it is these that I endeavour to expose, for these cannot be denied or bypassed.

Most of the prophecies from the past have been limited by the language and perceptions of the time in which they were passed on. For example, if I were to have seen the energy and image of a motor car within the collective potential of the human mind, a thousand years before the concept of such a vehicle had occurred or seemed possible to the general population on the ground, then how could I translate and explain this vision without a common frame of reference or the terminology to define what I had seen? With the limitations of that times language and perception of creation and the world, I might describe of having seen, "a shiny metallic monster, that roared along special stone tracks at high speeds, faster than any creature alive, and blew smoke from its tail." This is a crude way of exposing why so many prophecies of the past sound so bizarre and fantastical, and it is certainly not to say that all prophecies are based on true visions of the future, but it serves to get the point across. The few prophets that truly connected with the future of human potential, may have struggled to express the images of what they saw and felt, with the limited tools of their cultural language.

The experience of connecting with the collective mind and future potential of our evolution would have been an overpowering revelation in itself, and therefore what ever is translated from this experience may become extremely over exaggerated and flamboyant, making it very difficult to relate to ordinary day-to-day life. Also, as the awareness enters the more timeless state of spiritual potential where ideas are first developed and formed, it is very much like being in a dream state. As you merge and mix with the energy and concepts on this level, the images the mind pictures and may later translate to words, are often much more symbolic than literal.

Baring this in mind I make no illusions as to knowing time-scales or predicting dates for specific events during this process of transformation. I believe the Second Coming, the awakening of Christ consciousness throughout the whole human race, is a natural and gradual process: there will be moments of individual revelation and collective realisation, but in general, the awakening of Christ will take place (indeed is taking place) through our ordinary day-to-day lives and our experience of ourselves. It is unfolding in such a way that few may recognise its underlying reason, at least not until it has fulfilled its purpose.

I would suggest that if you are looking for the Second Coming, then look not for the emergence of a single Christ figure: a saviour to dazzle and romance you with miracles and to magic away all the bad in our world, rewarding only the good and righteous. But look instead within yourself, and ask yourself these questions: are you content with yourself...? Are you content with the world you live in...? Do you feel whole and free to express yourself...? Are you having to face fears within yourself...? Do you believe it is possible to live life in a better way...? Do you believe other people around the world are treated fairly...? Do you feel our present societies and systems of government are fair to all people, and offer us a happy sustainable future? And most importantly..., do you know what you are and why you are here...? It is here, in the answers to these questions, that you will find the return and awakening of Christ within your soul. For it is here, through you and your self-realisation, that this transformation is becoming a reality.

This awakening of Christ is already well underway, and as opposed to prophecy, this statement is more about the completion of an evolutionary process and the clarifying of its potential and purpose. Man's old relationship with the Universe has been broken down and superseded by a new one. Although the remnants of social dictatorships and repressive regimes still cause conflict in our world, today's collective balance lies with the human rights of the individual. The few systems of government and thought patterns that stand against this, are being progressively challenged and brought down. To a degree we have begun to realise the ideal of democracy and freedom in thought and expression, with only the personal conflicts of fear, ignorance and greed, the things that have shaped our highly commercial capitalist societies, denying its full realisation. This is reflected as man's relationship with each other and with the Universe reaches a more equal level: we have become individuals, no longer slaves, subjects, armies or followers.

Recently the doors to the free knowledge of the Universe began to open again. It has become the focus of our higher-self, with the collective consciousness of mankind being exposed to the truth of its past, present and potential future evolution. There are an immense amount of books and ideas that have been brought forward in recent years, each coloured with the unique experience of the individual souls that have presented them. This opening works, as with all things, according to the directives of the Universe, in co-operation and balance with human needs. It represents the dissolving and clearing of the dark veil of the Abyss within our collective consciousness, which in turn makes whole and reunites the nature of the human soul And this then releases the potential of our Christ nature to be fully exposed and eventually realised by the entire human race.

The clearing and dissolving of the Abyss has for some time been delicate and patient, but now increasingly becomes hard and uncompromising. In reality it means that each soul is being encouraged or forced to face its remaining fears and the entire accumulation of its unresolved karma, gathered throughout this time of decision, in a way so as not to push them over the edge. This is where our free will meets its limitations, for as this is a natural process of clearing and re-balancing, it is something that no soul can escape passing through. We each are exposed to the true reflection of all that we have given our life-force to over the years and centuries. All unresolved negative and destructive emotions are naturally drawn back to their originators to find balance, so that they can take responsibility for them, to learn and allow them to be cleared.

How we experience this process of exposure and clearing comes down to the balance of our soul and how we have directed our lives. If we have given life to following our instincts to evolve, to face and overcome our fears, relinquish the dominance of our animal nature, and take responsibility for and learn from our actions, then our soul will have little unresolved karma and will be strong and enlightened. This makes the crossing and clearing of the Abyss a welcome, easy, natural progression. On the other hand, if our soul has chosen to ignore its progressive instinct to evolve, and led many lives following self-interest, greed, abuse of others and violence, and has not taken responsibility for these actions to learn and grow from them. Then it will be facing the darkness of its fears and much unresolved karma and emotions. The clearing of the Abyss will reflect this, and in extreme cases where the soul is very weak and unprepared, it may be engulfed by the release of its karma and fear and unable to progress in this incarnation to reach the enlightenment of its true Christ nature.

If we were to look at this process from the old perceptions of God, then you might believe this to be God's judgement upon us: "These souls have been shown to be good by their deeds, they shall be rewarded with eternal life and shall inherit the Earth. These other souls have been shown to be bad by their deeds, they shall be punished and must suffer the consequences of their karma, which will destroy their life and end their time on Earth.". But what this 'judgement' actually means from a true Universal perspective is this:

The Universe has brought us to a point where we are now ready as a race to become aware of our true spiritual nature and identity, to realise our nature as soul entities, who's enlightened energy and unique experience of creation cannot be destroyed. This conscious realisation as a living human being exposes our eternal 'life' as soul entities, and not as the physical personality of one particular incarnation on Earth. As the doors to the Universe open, we are the channels to clear the unresolved negative emotions of the human race and thus raise our energy and awareness. All souls that have evolved towards their Christ nature, will be able to embody and progress through this transition, while those that have not evolved the strength to take these changes onboard, may experience the implosion of the self-destructive energy they have given life to (the clearing and balancing of their karma). This however is just a temporary experience that the soul will learn from, and certainly not an eternal damnation. It is an experience that will help the whole human race to learn, as it exposes to us all what becomes of repressing the soul's continued evolution.

As the weaker souls experience this clearing and opening, so the exposure may become too intense: the soul itself may withdraw from its incarnation and thus allow the unresolved fears and karma to engulf its personality and dissolve themselves, or 'burn' themselves out according to the fears and actions they reflect. Upon the ground it may appear to us that some people lose control of themselves and are taken over by their fear in some final destructive act. This may at times be very disturbing, as logical reasons as to why may elude us (this of course only applies to very extreme cases). But in reality this is a positive and necessary process, helping to clear the accumulated negative energy and karma within our collective consciousness, which at present denies us a clear understanding of the Universe and can create chaos and confusion in the collective mind. As the soul itself may not yet be ready or capable of realising its Christ nature, so it can carry forward what it has learnt from its experience on Earth and continue to evolve elsewhere in the Universe. Again the choices as to our actions are ours alone: we can let go and forgive ourselves, or we can be taken over by our destructive feelings.

In reality there are no 'good' or 'bad' souls, for the soul's central essence and nature is always light. There are just those that are ready to embody and expose Christ on Earth, and those that are not yet ready. The decision is not made by some superior being, or inside your personal mind, according to how you think you have behaved or whether or not you followed certain commandments. It is made according to the openness of your heart and the natural balance of your soul. There is no such thing as eternal damnation, or petty acts of anger and revenge by the Universe. This is just a primitive human perception of what we fear may happen. It is just that the Earth and the human race are moving on in their evolution and potential, and the opportunity to continue incarnating and learning on this same karmic level of experience will no longer be available. Souls that are not yet ready are not just discarded, the Universe maintains and develops souls according to their needs to evolve. Through need and attraction whatever experience is required already awaits, or is created and set up accordingly.

Far from being some great spectacular final judgement by God, the battle of Armageddon and the end of the world, the Second Coming represents the natural emergence of Christ consciousness throughout the whole human race. It is not about Jesus returning in the clouds, or demons climbing from the Abyss and destroying the Earth, or God ticking off the good and bad souls and casting them here or there. These are analogies based on fear, superstition and power; they symbolise our collective transformation and the individual conflict we may experience, but they are not literal definitions of the process. As I have said, nothing is written until it has come to pass; the opportunity to learn and take responsibility for life is there through each present moment. Whatever the future holds, the nature of the Universe is to progress and to evolve, to transfer potential into kinetic living reality and experience, and this is reflected in the primary nature and instinct of our own souls.

The signs of how this transition is affecting our lives upon the ground is most apparent within ourselves, in the unspoken questions of our own private minds and inner dialogue, and in the needs and callings of our own hearts. This then reflects in an unstable world, as old principles of government are destined to collapse in our rapidly changing modern societies. Whether conscious of it or not, collectively the whole human race is helping to open and clear the dark veil of the Abyss. Some more highly evolved souls have incarnated purely to support the process, while most are working through it to realise their Christ nature for the first time; no human stands outside of this experience.

The process of breaking down and clearing, works from both sides: our higher awareness, guided and supported by the Universe, works to bring down our karma and fears to our immediate consciousness, to encourage us to face this and release it, and thus consciously re-connect with the Universe and become more aware or our Universal nature. From the other side, upon the ground, we are the channels for this release and re-awakening. As individual personalities we must face and resolve our fears, deal with the karma of this and previous lifetimes, and learn to develop and express our own unique soul and its connection with the Universe.

This transformation works in a cyclic motion, like consecutive waves on the in-coming tide, energy carries forward karma which breaks on the surface of our daily lives and is dispersed. As more negative and destructive emotions and thought patterns are cleared, so the dark fog of the Abyss dissolves and more light passes through to reveal our true spiritual natures and to re-connect us with the consciousness of the Universe. Every soul is playing its part, and the more that connect with the Universe and become enlightened, then the clearer the collective mind becomes and the more exposed the remaining dark aspects of our natures are. This then forces the clearing of more karma, which in turn brings more light to the collective mind, and thus shifts the collective balance towards our Christ nature and soul enlightenment. While there may appear to be definite transitional phases and steps upon the ground, the process itself is completely fluid and on-going.

According to our past and present lives, individually and en masse, through all forms of collective identity (family, towns, cities, nations, religions, groups and sects), large amounts of unresolved karma and negative emotions are being released and cleared. This has resulted in aggressions, wars, breakdowns and breakthroughs; it is easy to ignore the positive that is coming forward as the negative so readily grabs our attention and is passed on through our media (something the doom mongers of prophecy like to shout about). In a sense we have become so accustomed to the way the world is, we just tend to take things for granted, and in many cases we are not aware of the true facts of what is going on. The process of opening and clearing the collective mind is now continual and on-going. It will not rest until the conscious reunion of body, mind and soul is complete for the whole human race, and all our dominant negative aspects are cleared, resolved and transcended.

As this clearing progresses, so more Universal truths are revealed and exposed. The rise of science and straight logical thinking has helped immensely to dissolve long held superstitions and fears, many of which were propagated by old religious orders seeking control. Old mysteries have been re-opened and re-examined, with new thoughts and theories being brought forward. Ancient wisdoms and practices have been revived, as our minds are curious to our past understanding of the Universe and our souls awake to their previous lives and experience. And this in turn helps us to re-evaluate and form a new clearer understanding of the Universe and our recent history.

Along side this there are souls and groups of souls who are making the transition to a more Universal level of awareness, who are developing and carrying forward new ideas and concepts of living. Throughout this period that we are presently immersed in, there have been breakdowns of previously held repressive social beliefs and codes of behaviour, and following these comes a flood of new ideas and inspirations that expand the imagination. Much of what first emerges can seem very impractical, as peoples minds can become disconnected with the grounded reality of the present day where there is still a great deal to be brought down and worked through to enable world wide transformation. Gradually the impractical is discarded by experience, and as feet come back to the ground, so new ways of living and thinking can be planted and nurtured. Our ideals can be like a balloon: once we grasp hold they can lift our feet off the ground and carry us away into the ether of our imaginations. To bring higher ideals and awareness back down to the ground, and to establish them as new ways of living, we then need to become strongly rooted in the present reality of our world. We need to accept the world as it is, to be able to change it and to introduce new practical ideals for living.

Many new ways of living and cults have sprung up in recent years, some just as superficial dabbling into ancient wisdoms, but they are all an early indication of the inner search for answers and truths that drives this transformation. Some cults can involve the resolving of karma for those involved, some help to expose the fears and superstitions of societies and organised religions, some may reflect a soul's affiliation with a particular wisdom or school of thought that has helped them to gain some enlightenment in a previous life, while others are quite simply new original creative ways of expressing a relationship with the Universe.

There are also many small communal ways of living being established: building on such ideals as greater self-sufficiency, barter and co-operation, recycling and renewable energy resources, and organic farming and the positive use of resources in balance with nature's ecosystems. They may not be mainstream as of yet, but they are working behind the scenes alongside our transformation and learning to incorporate all the knowledge, technology and wisdoms available, into their communities. I believe they are laying the early foundations for a whole new social structure to human societies.

At present it is still very much a case of trial and error for those souls that are awakening to their true potential, as some of the best lessons are learnt from making what may seem like mistakes at the time. All this experience and experimentation is helping to re-open the mind to the infinite possibilities of creation, and is leading each soul to the point of taking complete responsibility for its own evolution and so become self-realised. Just as with the few souls in the past that reached enlightenment, so each soul's experience becomes its own unique pathway to enlightenment and the nature of Christ; it is something that cannot truly be realised by imitating or following the pathway walked by another. In this respect each soul becomes the founder of its own unique religion, living life as an individual entity, yet forging a conscious union with the infinite mind of the Universe: seeing, feeling, thinking more as part of the collective.

For someone living and making their way through life in the present day, this can at times be a very hard, confusing and uncompromising reality; rest assured that the only anchor is in trusting your own heart and voice above all others. Life by definition is motion, and nothing is left to stagnate. We are increasingly compelled to make choices, to face the truth within ourselves and in the world we have created around us. The current future projections of our societies, based upon commercialism and our governments' economic policies, hold no sustainable future. This alone lies in the hands of evolution and in the human nature of Christ. We do all however have some degree of free will to choose our immediate direction: do we embody and go with our soul, or in our fear, repress and deny its future here on Earth...? Only you can decide for yourself, by your actions and not just your thoughts and wishes.

And so ends my own brief insight into more recent human evolution. As I have said, I tried to steer clear of specifying times and dates and going into the fine and complex details of our history. It is all too easy to become engulfed and lose track of the overall directives that have projected us through this time. My main aim has been to convey the simple concepts of our recent conscious evolution: how it is self- regulating, and that when it faced the obstacle of the destructive side of our fearing animal natures, how it naturally reacted and followed a diversionary course of evolution to evolve out the dominance of this aspect. This process represents the conscious transformation of human beings from primarily animal centred Earthly beings to spiritual centred Universal beings. It is a fluid on-going natural progression over a long period of time, that has definite overlapping stages where the collective focus of our evolution shifts.

First there is the recognition of the selfish part of our animal nature, a directive and primary instinct that served our earlier evolution and progression. Due to the cautious reaction of fearing the unknown, an instinct that had supported survival until now, a block was created to our further evolution as more open, exposed, collective spiritual beings. This then set in motion a whole diversionary experience for the human race to pass through, one that would gradually evolve out this dominant animal instinct to replace it with the open and sensitive Universal instinct of love.

Having clarified these needs, so the process gradually became our reality, and began with the **'Fall from grace'**. As our awareness had already begun to connect with the energy and creative power of the Universe, so the energy potential at our disposal was awesome. Because of the imbalance caused by our selfish ego nature, this potential was not always being used in balance with the Earth's nature and needs. The fall from grace represents the gradual regression of our awareness from its connection with and knowledge of the Universe, so as to limit the energy and potential available to the human race while this inner conflict was resolved.

As this regression of awareness took place, so the **'Construction of the Abyss'** began within the collective consciousness of humanity. The Abyss is an illusory veil of darkness used to conceal our higher awareness of the rest of the Universe and creation from our immediately accessible consciousness. This then encloses our remaining awareness and consciousness upon the Earth to pass through the experience of its potentially destructive nature, and thus overcome these instincts. Crossing or passing through this veil of the Abyss, requires an individual to overcome its animal fear of the unknown and put their evolutionary need to learn and progress first. This real experience of stepping into the unknown darkness of our consciousness, and passing through to reach enlightenment and to connect with our Universal awareness, reflects exactly the experience we need to evolve beyond our fearing animal natures. It then replaces these instincts with love and faith: for all true faith is, is a trust in the providence of the Universe through need and attraction, that comes from the experience of letting go of our animal survival instincts.

Once the Abyss was constructed, then the individual souls of the human race were ready to be exposed to their true potential as spiritual beings, and from then on left to experience the dark side of their nature and to learn to evolve beyond this. This represents the first full **'Exposure of Christ'**, which is the Universal awareness we all evolve towards, and it marks the turning point in our regression. Our remaining consciousness is now encapsulated and ready to pass through the experience of its dark side, having been exposed to its future potential and advised of the pitfalls along the way.

After the exposure of Christ we are left to pass through a **'Time of Decision'**, a period of time where each soul learns to be responsible for its own evolution and actions. We are able to choose the circumstances of our incarnations, to bring forward and face our fears, and to take responsibility for and learn from our actions. Many lifetimes are available to learn: different times, cultures, traditions, families, relationships, are all made available to help our progression, and we are free to choose how much or how little to work through, supporting and helping each other along the way.

As this time of decision nears an end, so begins the **'Second Coming'** of Christ. Gradually the Abyss is broken down and cleared and the full expanse of our human awareness is reunited and revealed: all past wisdoms and future potentials. Our fearing animal instincts are removed with the clearing of the Abyss: those souls that can let go of these pass through and carry forward the future evolution of the human race and the Earth, to live from their Christ awareness and become living spiritual beings... While those that are unable to let go, move on to continue their evolution elsewhere.

And so the transition will be made complete. I do not ask you to believe what I have written here, nor do I expect your acceptance of these ideas, the only thing I advocate is the freedom of the individual to find their own answers. I hope that this may help to provoke or stimulate some thought as to who we are, why we are here, and where we are going.

The Logic Of Living In The Present

Time is completely fluid, a continual motion of energy, transformed from spiritual potential into the kinetic motion and reality that we call life. We however, tend to divide time into moments and periods, according to how we direct the spiritual energy and consciousness that is continually flowing through us and enabling us to evolve. One moment we may be engrossed in thought within our own minds, while the next we may be talking to someone and connecting with their mind, and the next we may be preparing some food, eating, or seeing to some other physical necessity. Our whole life is a series of moments and time periods, connected through consciousness and following one after another, fluctuating between internal thought and analysis and external expression and action. Each present moment is an act of creation, where our potential to think, act and evolve is made real.

Having experienced an overview of our creation and our direction in evolution, I now look to bring my feet firmly back to the ground, and to commit my entire being to living in the present. When I look at the world outside revolving in its daily cycles, it can at times seem daunting and unmoved by the reality of our transformation, or at least endeavour to give that impression. Occasionally in the past the fleeting thought of, "is it all worth it?" has passed through my mind, but I now find my soul relentless in its pursuit of clearing negative energy and karma and revealing truth. My view of the world is no longer dictated by the images I see portrayed on the surface, or by the influences of anyone else's beliefs, which is not however to say it doesn't share common agreement with other people. My view is born of my own heart and mind, from the perspective of an individual human being, living as part of an evolving Universe that is formed of an infinite potential of conscious energy.

The world we have created for ourselves is the way it is: it can be ignorant, destructive, cruel and painful at times..., just as it can be loving, creative, joyful and wonderful. I see my only true responsibility, indeed capability, is to be true to myself and live from my heart as the natural being that I am. This is the only thing that is truly within my hands, so in all honesty I can be or do nothing else. If I do not begin by accepting the World the way it is in the present, then how can my being here effect a change. Things are the way they are for a reason, I do not need to judge, fight or condemn anything. In this I have realised the simplicity of life, just to be myself and to follow my heart, for this alone offers the greatest power and support within the collective, and thus is the greatest tool to bring about change and progression. This is an outline of my own personal perception of the world we live in today, a world that is continually progressing and changing....

Our human societies are composed of living, breathing individuals: souls incarnated into the biological organism that is the human body, each with their unique personality and life, and each with a slightly different level of awareness. Together they compose our collective thinking and balance as a race, and this forms the foundation upon which our present social morals, laws and governments are developed and upheld. All such laws and ideals, whether based on religious commandments, philosophical meditations, or the voting strategies of a political party, exist only as an outline to enable basic stability and human rights within a society. Ultimately there is no Universal 'right' and 'wrong', simply because we evolve and learn from experience. We decide these things for ourselves as individuals, according to the balance of our human nature and the reactions of our conscience.

So for example, sometimes the use of violence is right in the sense that it expresses the overpowering instinct that someone may feel, and only after the experience can they learn from the whys and wherefores. Far from condoning destructive actions or being offended or repulsed by them, this view accepts their reality and looks to understand the reasoning behind them; a pattern that repeats itself can only begin to be broken down once we understand why it has come to be in the first place. In this respect, condemning and fighting with violence what we perceive as injustice, offers little resolution to why it occurs in the first place.

So what do we consider to be an injustice? An offence against our human rights perhaps. And how do we define our human rights? For within these lies the present focus of our evolutionary needs and directives. Well to me, our most basic human rights lie in these foundations and are accorded by our birth into human nature: the right to live freely on the Earth and provide for our self, our family and our community, the basic necessities of sustaining life: food, water and shelter... The right to free thought and expression within the society we live, so that ideas can be explored, expanded and realised... And finally the right to feel that we alone possess and direct our life, even if we feel we must end it, should we so wish... Provided we do not impose upon or deny the rights of others in pursuit of these, then no other foundations for law are needed, for these are the present directives of our nature, taking us beyond the old, 'survival of the fittest' and 'eye for an eye and tooth for a tooth' judgements.

Now the last of these human rights may seem a strange thing to say, and would probably not make most people's list, but it is my belief that the very taboo of considering death or taking one's own life, often leads people to suicide without first considering the consequences, or trying to regain some positive perspective to life. As humans, the one thing we posses as our own, is our life, and if we do not feel we have the freedom to take that away from ourselves, then how can we truly appreciate what it is we would lose, and so come to posses it for everything that it is? Life is a wonderful gift, it is ours, but if we are to lose this perspective, then it can seem like a prison sentence at times. And this is the feeling that has driven many to an unnecessary suicide. I am certainly not advocating suicide to people, quite the opposite, but I believe there are few people alive that have not considered it within themselves at some point in life, not because they want to go through with it, but because their human nature is curious, and this is the one consideration that can offer a deep and resounding reflection as to what our life means to us. We use this consideration at times to trim away all the rubbish and confusion we pick up and carry within our minds. If we were free to consider and talk about death more, then I believe that few people would feel the need to go through with suicide, as life could be brought back to some true perspective before an act of desperation takes place.

Of course there are other ways our right to end our life can be seen as a basic human right. Euthanasia is a major example: the fact that some people are denied the means to an easy and peaceful death when suffering immense pain, is an imposition upon their basic human rights. There are many arguments against euthanasia (like what if a cure were to be found for their illness..., or who are we to play God..., or who can be expected to administer the treatment and take responsibility), but none of them change the fact that to be denied the freedom of choice as to what you would want to do with your life, takes responsibility away and opposes your human rights. No matter what anyone else says or believes, I have the right to end my own life should I feel it to be the most desired course of action, and in acknowledging this, I alone can embrace and posses this life I lead. For anyone to oppose or deny me that right, just exposes how little we still understand about death and how much we still fear its inevitable reality.

And what of the other two primary human rights: the right to live and provide for ourselves and the right to freely express ourselves. As long as we are free to follow these rights and we do not take more than our basic needs require or deny the rights of others, to take their resources and hurt or kill them, then these stand as our basic human birth rights. These rights are founded upon the evolutionary directives of individual responsibility. Most of the modern laws of our governments and societies can be traced back to these basic rights, while some of the older ones are still based on fear and religious superstition. Yet if we take an honest look at the world we live in today, how unequally our resources are divided and the needs of different peoples and cultures are catered for, it becomes all too clear just how much our basic human rights are still opposed and denied throughout the world today. Two simple reasons for this come to mind and they are both the result of human fear: ignorance and greed. Ignorance of the nature of the Earth and the needs of others, and the greedy desire to have, posses and experience much more than we truly need to live and prosper. It is only these two aspects of human nature that deny the realisation of a truly collective and prosperous human race, one that respects completely the human rights of every individual.

So let's start by taking a closer look at the governing principle of democracy: by definition it is, **1** a system of government by the whole population (usually through elected representatives), **2** a **classless** and tolerant form of society (favouring social equality). Few places, if any as of yet, have been able to realise this form of democracy. In reality, as individual voters, what we are offered is the choice of a few traditional parties, each with their manifestos and pledges, that have the organisation and financial backing to advertise themselves to the general population and stand for a government election. The system at present lacks real and sustained involvement from the general public, most of whom are busy trying to sustain a living and maintain a home and family, leaving little time for new political thought and involvement. Every so often we are fed varying degrees of information from the established political parties, and are then asked to apply a cross after the party we most agree with on one particular day. From then on, the party with the majority of seats forms its own government, and has the power to dictate social policy and law for the rest of that society during its allotted time in office. Whether it continues to appreciate the needs of the people or not is up to its elected members and representatives, and their ability to truly listen.

We as individuals have little involvement beyond the pre-election campaigning and the casting of a vote; a system that suits the majority of candidates at present, as whether or not they get voted into office depends largely upon the image they portray to the public, as opposed to their true motivation and their desire to serve the public's needs. We of course are partly responsible, as voting traditions are passed down through families, regardless of what a political party can achieve for a nation. Often there is a feeling of disinterest: people can see through the pre-election promises of politicians desperate to gain power, they have learnt from experience and may believe that there is little their single isolated vote can do to effect change.

Today's societies demand so much time and effort to sustain a living and offers so many distractions to free independent thinking, there is little time and energy left to debate politics and create and implement new ideas for government. Many of those who choose to follow political careers, whether conscious of the fact or not, seek the power of office. We have a steep political stepladder, that tends to wear down honest idealism and hold back people primarily motivated by the desire to serve the public good, deploying them else where in a party. Hard and ruthless personal ambition is often the way to the top, and such selfish determination rarely makes for good genuine listeners. The basic commercial and industrial nature of social economics, upon which our governments are founded, seems to have been accepted as 'just the way it is'. The minimal differences in party policy is just about how you propose to govern these resources and how much you take and give back to the rich, poor and middle classes.

Much of the party political advertising and the thoughts that have come to decide our voting, aim at personal wealth: "How much better off will I be? Which party is offering me the best deal?" Many of the fundamental issues of government, relating to human rights, ecological respect, our purpose and direction as human beings, tend to be ignored or taken for granted. This gives a clear indication as to what calls the shots in our present political thinking. We have come to equate prosperity simply with the measure of personal wealth: how much we can buy, consume and own as individuals. If we look at the direction and purpose of our present systems of government and ask the all-important questions: "What is their purpose...? Where are they leading us as a race...? What sort of world will our children inherit if we continue in this direction...?", then I wonder what our honest answers would be.

Basically we are going round in circles: commercialism is the driving force and personal wealth the main aim. Science and engineering are mostly directed towards creating ever more refined, specified and aesthetically pleasing mod cons and gadgets, and to discovering and utilising the energy resources necessary to drive the wheels of industry. These products then can be marketed and mass produced, and blanketly advertised to the population; made to seem desirable and necessary to our lives. The general population, according to their developed abilities, their desire for personal wealth, and their needs to support themselves and a family, then seek an employed position within this chain. Few of us actually have the provisions to own our own homes (most officially belong to the banks and mortgage companies), or to be self-sufficient in providing food, water and shelter. Hence we are forced to work for the majority of our lives, often in a job we may not be completely happy with, to reach a position of relative financial security. For the most part we evolve and change superficially with the adaptation of technology and the changes of fashion. We fill our lives and homes with the mod cons that our consciousness has been 'image' bombarded with almost since birth. Within such a complex and sometimes chaotic social structure there is little personal time and space for self-discovery and freethinking. These impulses are mostly repressed, and they certainly are not commonly advertised as the way to a secure future, not unless there is money to be made.

This cycle of thinking is introduced at an early age: subliminally we absorb it from birth, and then our education systems, the limited subject matter of which is proposed by government, teach us that this cycle is what life is all about.

They work on a system of praise and reward, and as our parents have been taught in this fashion and have learnt from experience that personal wealth leads to better physical security in the short term, so they pass this thinking on, naturally wanting the best for their children. Our present education systems are extremely imbalanced, in that they pressurise children from an early age into retaining large amounts of information, and to reproduce it when asked, under the unnatural conditions of test and examination. It focuses on and rewards the types of intellect that would support and propagate a commercial society, while artistic gifts, sensitivity, idealism, are only given token attention. Even children with physical and athletic gifts are channelled towards competitive and commercial sport from an early age. Those without the desired intellects or sporting prowess, are offered little hope for the future. Many are brushed aside and ignored, becoming dependants of the state, or turning to crime to taste some of the elixir of personal wealth that they have been brainwashed with. And so the foundations of this early conditioning and education, coupled with the mental absorption of continual advertising imagery, sends another generation out into the world to continue the cycle.

The soul however cannot be repressed indefinitely. We are learning from this experience and becoming saturated by it. The cracks have been showing for many years now and leaks are springing forward in every direction. I have heard a lot of talk over the years about today's younger generation, mostly coming from older generations: 'they are not performing well enough at school..., standards are dropping..., they have no respect..., there is too much truant and bad behaviour...' But today's young generation can carry a heavy burden. We have divorced them from discovering and knowing the true value of things in the overabundance of our commercial societies, that can serve to devalue communities and even families. Many children are raised by children themselves; they are constantly shown the abundance of our commercial world and made to think they need this. Children have become the most common target of commercial advertising, yet rarely are they educated as to the true costs of our present overabundance.

And those children that do not have the required skills to carve their career within this commercialism, and thus claim their high salaries…, well they are offered, from an early age, little if any hope for a prosperous future. Children who cry out loud are only expressing their feelings, feelings that obviously can no longer be repressed; it falls to them to help to break this cycle and bring back the joy to education. Education needs free expression and self-discovery as its priorities, to enable the soul to breath again, and children to respect and appreciate what they can learn and pass on. It is not a case of condoning bad behaviour, truancy, violence, crime and drug abuse, for these are the signs and symptoms of our imbalanced and greedy societies. It is a case of understanding why these things arise and what they express. Our present education systems have run their course, we have learnt from them and now need to move forward, to open and adapt. Few children are deceitful enough to deny their emotions; how they say something is usually honest with what they feel, and they demand more say in their education and more hope for the future. All we need to do is listen and read the signs.

I am certainly not presenting what some might see as a conspiracy theory: denying people information, manipulating thinking, twisting the truth, and opposing freethinking. But our societies have grown (consciously and subconsciously) to come to occupy our minds at all times: thoughts of a career, future, birthdays, Christmas, holidays, mortgages, investments, pensions, bills, taxes, weddings, funerals, TV, sports, hobbies, food, and in the case of a lot of third world countries, just the daily struggle to survive and feed your family. Our minds are so awash with the ways of the world, that we are afforded little time for anything else, and so the cycle continues. We may not be happy with the way things are, we may wish for a better way of life, but many of us tend to believe there is little we can do, so we make the best of things the way they are. Good intentions abound, and our true wholistic spiritual nature that draws us towards love, cannot be repressed forever. Behind this all still lies the same simple root and block that obstructs the way ahead, the fear that has given life to human greed.

Greed has evolved from being blatant and obvious, in the all-conquering attitude that simply killed and took what it pleased, to naturally assimilate with our societies and systems of government. It has clothed and concealed itself within religion and politics, more subtly manipulating to achieve its aims: controlling thinking, monopolising markets, creating dependencies. In the present day our societies are saturated by greed: the western philosophies that uphold commercialism and industrialisation as the 'right' way ahead for our economic based societies, have gradually sought to seize hold of the natural resources of the planet. These are then used to fuel the industrial and technological cycle, often at the expense of ecosystems, animals, forests, indigenous tribes and cultures, the environment in general.

Other developing nations and third world countries are advised and encouraged to follow suit. Our governments and banks lend and invest money into them, giving them our systems of democracy and education. Many are used and abused by our western nations, under the pretext of giving them a better standard of living. They are raped of their natural resources, their peoples are used as cheap and expendable (slave) labour, to mass produce the overabundance of commercial goods we see on our shop floors and shelves, while many of them struggle to feed and clothe themselves and their families. We have helped to wipe out much of their traditional culture and roots and made them dependent, helping to seriously damage or even destroy the environments that once sustained them.

Our media is obsessed with the money markets and shares, as if these were central to our existence, and they are saturated with advertising strategies and logos. Our politics offers positions of power, and therefore attracts those who seek power, and seek to control thinking and resources. From this we have seen scandal after scandal of personal greed and deceit emerging within politics and big business. In all truth, our present systems of government and economic policies, remain where they are, simply to allow some people to take more than others: they justify one person receiving a salary 10, 100, 1000 times grater than another, simply because his intellect works in a different way, and he or she can work further up the chain of commercialism. We live in a world where the peoples of one nation can suffer from obesity, eating disorders and over consumption..., while the peoples of another nation are starving to death. Even as I write these words, or as you are now reading them, someone, somewhere in the world is dying of a heart attack brought on by excessive diet, while another, somewhere else, is breathing their last few weak breaths as they die of starvation. That is the extremity of division we have created in our modern world.

Admittedly this paints a rather bleak view of our present societies, but it does help to expose the challenges we are presently having to face, resolve and work through; it challenges us to take responsibility. I am not saying these things are good or bad, because they are all part of our learning, and if you take a look around, you can see that people are responding and things are changing. New political parties and ideals are being presented, new ideas to education are being proposed, charities and aid organisations are helping people to help themselves. There is a collective shift towards uncovering and facing the truths of our present societies, and taking responsibility for our actions. History is being re-written from a more honest perspective, while in the present we are forced to be more honest with ourselves, and to take more responsibility for our actions.

It is a simple fact that we have enough resources, if managed fairly and used in balance with the Earth's natural environment and ecosystems, to comfortably sustain the world's population and uphold their human rights. If our priority in government was truly democracy, to offer a fair share to all the people according to their needs, then our social economic structures would be co-operative and not competitive. We have the technology to inform and involve general populations in important government decision making, of the kind that will affect our lives, using TV, radio, the Internet and computer web sites for example. We do not need the over-abundance of food, clothes and technological appliances we manufacture, to sustain a comfortable and stable lifestyle. The resources that are poured into these things could easily be redirected into solving our humanitarian problems, and into building strong sustainable communities. Only our greed and our fear of change stops us from making use of these simple facts.

Despite the negative element of all I have written about greed, this whole world reality and present human experience, provides us with the greatest of lessons. Greed is what we need to understand within our nature and to overcome, so greed is what we are experiencing. We have begun and will continue to experience the repercussions of our ignorance to the environment, of our abuse of people and their humanity, of our greed that hoards possessions only to lose them later in life. From this whole experience we will learn, and we will overcome our propensity towards greed and evolve beyond, of this I have no doubts whatsoever.

When we break down the 'sophisticated' expressions and traditions our greed has come to represent, from the size of our house, car, bank balance, the number of holidays we can afford, the price of an antique or famous piece of art, to the number of pieces of cutlery at our dining table… When we trace this back to its origin…, all that stares back at us, is a frightened animal, puffing out its chest, desperate to survive and seem big. This alone is what drives people to view themselves and be viewed as a class above others. For them, this justifies taking and hoarding ridiculous amounts of wealth, only to have to part with it and face once more their physical mortality. In the present day the merciless and uncompromising face of business, is portrayed as strong and admirable, the way to get ahead; it is almost accepted as an icon... And yet all it continues to expose is the weak, fearing animals that we still choose to be.

When I was a child I had a thought that I was quite proud of at the time, and I wondered why no one had thought of it before: "If so many people are poor, then why not just print more money and give it to them?" Of course when I said this out loud it was the cause of some laughter, and I was told I was naïve. But no one could really explain why it was so funny, "it just doesn't work like that" they said. More recently that thought has returned to me, and I have come to realise that it is not as silly as it may first seem. The reason why nobody could explain to me why this idea was so funny, was simply because very few people actually know how our monetary system works and upon what basis we print and distribute money.

Without going too far back into its history, money originated as a common substitute for direct barter and the exchange of goods; it came to represent the physical resources and skills we had to offer. This then evolved over the years into the foundations of our present monetary system (at least up until 1971), that of the 'gold exchange standard' regulated by the US dollar. This system has had to adapt and change, into a federal reserve system, to include other categories of money (the most common of which is M1, which consists of currency and demand deposits, the most easily liquidized forms of money). The gold exchange standard basically worked according to this: a country's wealth, and therefore their ability to print and circulate money and trade with other countries, is measured by the amount of gold they posses (and of course other valuable metals and natural resources, that can be converted to money) or the number of U.S. dollars they have to exchange for gold, regardless of where the gold originally came from or how it was obtained.

Ironically enough this exchange standard was recently forced to change and include other categories of money, because it turned out that the amount of money that had been printed and circulated over the years, was over five times more than the gold stock it represented (so much for naive ideas). It wasn't that there weren't enough resources to go round and that people were forced to be poor, it was just that they had not found and laid claim to, or fought for these resources, and were therefore deemed to have no rights to the money that was printed in their representation. This alone is what the divide between our peoples and nations, and their apparent wealth, is based upon.

To me, from this perspective, it seems like a most childish and primitive system: it is like saying, "Well I have acquired more of this shiny non-corrosive yellow metal than you, therefore I can print more money and buy and consume more of the things I desire...., and if you don't posses, or weren't quick enough to lay claim to any of these resources, then you and your people will just have to go without and starve. If you have a problem with that, I have a big army and lots of imaginatively destructive weapons (paid for with all the money I have accumulated) to back me up." The resource of a human being is not even taken into consideration, apart from being the source of labour to extract these resources.

If you don't have something considered as valuable to fuelling our present economies, then frankly you are worthless. If you look at our third world countries, some of these have or at least had, large amounts of gold and / or natural resources, so how is it that they are not among the wealthiest nations of today, and that many of their peoples struggle to make a living? In most cases it is the large industrial corporations and banks of the western world who are responsible: they have sought to manipulate these developing nations and third world countries, by offering money and support to the governments in power. Once they have won favour they then bring in and set up their industries, draining and mining the country's natural resources and using their people as cheap expendable labour. This of course is done under the pretext that what they bring in to the country will bring stability and democracy. It will offer jobs, money and prosperity to the people, giving them a better standard of living, and it will help them to develop quickly and become a political and economic power in their own right.

In reality these actions are no different from the marauding and colonisation's that blatantly exposed our greed in the past, only now the marauders come dressed in suits and ties as our friends, smiling, shaking hands and baring gifts. The peoples of the third world have been used and abused, just because they did not need nor recognised the importance of their natural resources and had not laid claim to them (gold or oil is not exactly a necessity for a tribal existence). So they have been stolen, drained and used by our greedy industrial nations, for very little in return. Tribal cultures and ecosystems have been destroyed, environments damaged, people have been made dependent on industries that care little about their livelihoods: they pay extremely little for long working hours, and if resources run out or a cheaper work force can be found else where, so they can just pack up and move on.

So the western governments and their industries brought with them Western democracy, but this is still controlled by greed and finance and can merely escalate what may already be an unstable and volatile political situation. And they have brought and sold on western weapons of destruction, under the pretext that these make a nation more powerful and therefore more secure, but these can only increase the insecurities and casualties of war (an extremely profitable money making exercise, especially for the Western nations that manufacture arms). And they have brought us Western medicine and health care, under the promise of wiping out and curing diseases, but while this is true in the cases of some illnesses and a better standard of health care has been achieved, Western medicine has also brought new problems: the Westerners that first came to these countries introduced new diseases, ones that the indigenous peoples had no resistance to, and thus many have died from these illnesses. Second, as the health care was gradually increased, so populations rose with lower mortality rates, and the natural ecological balance of populations was disturbed. More people were born and lived, so more demands were put upon a fragile environment (coupled with the industrial destruction). Lands were over worked and drained of nutrients, while forests were cleared for farming, thus disturbing the ecosystems and natural cycles even further. This coupled with the global affects of domestic and industrial pollution upon the Earth's natural weather cycles, has led to crops failing and large populations spiralling into mass famine. The majority of third world countries that have been lent money and invested in by our Western banks and businesses, under the promise of a 'better way of life', are now left, on paper, owing thousands and millions in debt and interest. They have no capability of ever paying this back, not least because their natural resources have been drained or taken over by the Western run companies and banks that they are supposedly indebted to.

Again this does all sound a little bit bleak, but it helps us to see and experience the manipulative and destructive nature of human greed; this is how we have chosen to learn and how we are forced to take responsibility. The positive reaction to these abuses is sustained by the human spirit and is therefore stronger than any multi-national company or bank: it is indestructible. It gains momentum with every day as the truth is exposed and people come together in a common cause of good. Lands and resources are being reclaimed, and people are joining together to stand up for their human rights. When people are no longer deceived by greed, then it can be recognised for what it is, and it can be overcome...

Throughout this life I have often heard people use the saying that, "Money is the root of all evil", but how can this be possible? Money is completely inanimate, it is just a man-made commodity, a medium to ease the trade of goods essential for life. It has become all to easy to redirect the blame on to something that cannot speak in its own defence, for in all honesty it is plain for all to see that human greed alone is at the root of all our evils. The extreme survival instinct that desires to have more and more, regardless of how it gets it or where it comes from.

Money is just a medium; it represents the value we assign to the natural resources around us, and it enables us to buy and sell these resources across the globe, between all nations, colours and creeds. Traced back to its origins, money is just a concept, born and delivered into use by humankind. Without people to locate, mine, compound and redesign these resources, they remain untouched within the Earth. In this respect the ultimate resource we have is us, human beings. People are the true resource, and as such, we hold the power for directing the changes that take place and the way ahead. It is the worker that creates the product that brings money to the greedy directors and share holders (greedy in the sense that the majority of these do very little and then take vast amounts more then they need to live, simply because they are in a position to do so, and if others suffer because of this, then it becomes a criminal offence against their human rights). And it is the buyer that allows production to continue, and thus improves the bank balance of the directors and shareholders.

In reality, those who have the determination or inherited finances to seek out or create a position within our economical cycles, to siphon off the majority of the wealth created by the hard work of the labourers, whether at the expense of our homes, environments, third world countries, or even lives in some cases..., only continue to do so because we allow them to. We facilitate this process, and whether conscious of the fact or not, many of us look up to this icon of greed, always wanting more for ourselves. We continue to vote in forms of government that support this social and economic structure, and we have not yet given the time, the belief, or the energy to change this reality, and to imagine and implement new fairer ideas and systems of government. It is the individuals who join together in a common cause, with strength and perseverance, that have the power to change anything within the present reality of our world, and thus bring about the reality of change.

If we were to take all the time and energy, all the creativity and life force, directed into the juvenile folly of commercialism and advertising, and the paranoid creation of weapons of mass destruction, armies and war, and these were to be re-directed into confronting and resolving the many problems and imbalances within our societies, and to creating and implementing a fair democratic system of world government, based on the co-operation of all nations and the respect of everyone's human rights and needs.... Then I believe it would only be a matter of years before we started reaping the rewards. You can after all only reap what it is that you sow.

Just step back and look for one minute at the immensity of energy and resources poured into TV and satellite marketing, sports and sponsorship, company advertising and logos..., all aiming to imprint themselves within our already complicated minds. Try to imagine the day-to-day energy that is spent on war research, weapons production, armies, navies, and air forces, not to mention the wars that are at this moment being fought. Imagine all of this energy combined and re-directed to positive humanitarian causes, and then just think what could be achieved. The hard part is not to build a new fairer and more peaceful world; with this amount of energy and people almost anything can be achieved. The hardest part is changing the present system that we have become so accustomed to..., and the only thing we need to remove to allow this to happen, is the fear that has led us to become greedy.

We then are responsible, each and every one of us: before anything can change we have to decide what we truly feel for life, we have to know ourselves. So do we continue to measure prosperity in terms of personal wealth, believing this offers the greatest security for ourselves and our families? From my own experience and view of the world, this creates a fractionated society of classes that is closed, competitive and insecure. Or do we look to imagine a greater reality? For this can only be achieved through total belief and commitment. If the prosperity of society were measured by the health and happiness of all its people, as opposed to their accumulated personal wealth, then where would we stand in the present day? It seems simple logic to me, and is proved by the very fact that we have come to form societies, that the best interests of the community offers the greatest stability. Here society can be open, co-operative and supporting to the individual; the many working together can achieve far more than the individual working alone.

The logic of this does all sound very simple on paper, but our present reality and day-to-day experience of life, can at times seem harsh and mundane. The present systems of society tend to propagate the impression and thinking that, " this is the way it has been for so long, and this is the way it will go on.": it seems that the same people pass us by on the way to work, the same factories churn out their goods, the same cars fill the roads and motorways (with the continual addition of a few more), the same advertisements pop up on the TV... It can almost be comforting to hide in this world of diversity we have created. But it simply isn't true that our world and its societies are that stable: the false ethics of commercialism and its fuel supplies are dwindling and the natural weather patterns and ecosystems that sustain us are changing drastically in a short space of time. One day soon, ready or not, change is going to hit your day-to-day life, if it hasn't already, and you will be forced to think again. Industrialisation has not been around for that long; it is not that we truly believe things can continue this way indefinitely, it is that we kid ourselves for now and look the other way, waiting for someone else to make the moves, or just hiding in the complexities of our day-to-day lives.

To those who have already looked beyond the present ways of society, to believe in something better, then the desire to bring about change can at times be an extremely frustrating and painful reality. Governments and large corporations have taken hold of the land upon which we live and written their own laws and deeds of ownership. If you wish to begin to create and live by your own co-operative lifestyle, and to come together through shared beliefs with other like minded souls, then where do you go without the resources to buy the land back that you would need to support yourselves? Sustaining a living in the present day can leave little time and energy for thoughts of self-discovery, or the inspiration of new ideas, and it can at times seem almost impossible to effect any change in thinking.

But this is never really true. As our sole responsibility is with ourselves and how we live our lives, so it is that change is initiated and carried forward through ourselves. Each one of us supports and affects the collective mind: the more we advocate a lifestyle of open-mindedness and free thinking, then the more this is supported within the collective mind and the more it is opened up. We don't have to change anybody else's mind, or fight against greed or ignorance, we only need to open and set free our own minds. No matter how small we may think the knock-on effect will be within the collective, we all play our part. As your inner strength and enlightenment grows, so the effect and support for change increases. It is a simple and natural process. We need only have the faith and commitment to set free and open our own minds and to live from the true nature of our hearts, to speak out for and follow our highest ideals. This will then help to expose the fearful nature of greed (no matter where it hides) and will help to transform human nature to a new level of collective awareness and co-operation.

On every level of energy and consciousness, right down to the physical reality of our present day lives and personalities, the Universe provides what we need. It has created everything and we are inseparable from its intelligence, its love, and its evolutionary directives. As we open our minds and begin to follow our hearts, so we begin to hear and speak according to the voice of our soul, and hence we are guided directly by need and attraction: what we need to survive or to learn, will either come to us or we will be drawn to it. Education by experience is the only true form of learning; this is why we have incarnated, to evolve from experience. Ultimately, whatever path your life follows offers some form of learning, there are no right or wrong ways as to how to become enlightened.

Fear and excitement are the two natural instincts we can feel when faced with the unknown. They produce identical effects upon the body: the raise in the heart beat, the vigorous increase of blood pumped around the body, the alerting of the senses. Both give a feeling of intensity to being alive. These two reactions represent the two possible states of mind with which we can face the unknown, the doorway to change and new experience. Fear reflects the desire to turn away, to run and hide and bury the head in the safety of what we already know and are accustomed to, and if you cannot run then you must destroy that which threatens. Excitement on the other hand, reflects the desire to step forward and embrace the unknown, to jump in and give light to new experience and ideas. I hope that at least some of what I have written here will help to expose fear for what it is, and in doing so, transform the future of what lies ahead into something immensely exciting. Whatever the future holds, our eternal soul will be a part of it, and everything that we have lived will remain always, imprinted eternally within the Universe's self-realisation.

Possibilities Of The Future

While I have already voiced my belief that nothing is written until it becomes an experienced reality, there is immense potential that lies ahead of us as a race, as we begin to merge consciously with the energy and intelligence of the Universe. Too strong a focus on the future can only serve to draw you away from living and working in the present. However, it is something I have been instinctively drawn to contemplate at times; it helps to regenerate hope and to intensify the focus and resolve to work within the present. These are just a few of the general ideas that have come forward in my own mind as I have contemplated and been carried into our future. There are undoubtedly many others and I'm sure that each person will have their own particular projections. Many of these ideas are with us today in their early stages of growth, and as the predominance of our animal natures is superseded by the open spiritual instinct of unconditional love, so these realities may flower and bare fruit.

As we move towards a much more collective and co-operative human race, overcoming our self-defensive instincts and fears, then the threat of war and violence will no longer be used to resolve our differences. Open discussion and debate is quickly becoming a common everyday tool for airing views and resolving problems, right down to the most mundane levels of reality TV. Respect for the human rights and opinions of others is progressively being learnt and appreciated, and this is helping to expose and break down long held prejudices and superstitions. As we move into the future, so this respect for human rights and free expression will become central to our societies and governments; without the self-interest of greed, people can appreciate the needs and reasoning of the other side of a disagreement, allowing differences to be resolved peacefully and amicably.

As our energy and awareness is raised in its consciousness, so we become much more sensitive to different energy levels and spiritual emanations. Our five physical senses will become much more finely tuned and sensitive, leading to the common acceptance and use of our sixth intuitive sense. Energy auras will become more open and brighter, and will be much more easily detected by sight and touch, and thought waves will become 'louder' and more powerful. All our senses will develop the ability to detect and communicate with things on an energy level, merging with and embracing the whole being of something, as opposed to relying upon the personal interpretation of one or more perceived physical senses.

When we project this increased sensitivity upon the conscious mind, so we begin to see the accelerated development of new types of communication. Telepathy is already in its early stages of development within our human nature. It is already much more common an experience than we might at present realise, but it still works on such a subtle level between our minds, that we are rarely aware of the experience. In the present, thoughts and mind waves pass between people all the time, interacting and communicating, sometimes across vast distances. These may be very weak and faint in most cases, but whenever you look upon or think upon another person, then thoughts are being transferred. Take as a simple example two people in conversation: the conversation goes quiet for a moment, one person thinks of something to say or a question to ask, but before they have voiced this thought the other person picks up on it and says the same thing, or answers their question. It's quite a common occurrence, but at present most telepathy takes place on a very subtle and often superficial level, when we are in a completely relaxed and casual state of mind. The problem with testing telepathy is that if we try to read thoughts, we tend to strain and constrict the mind and its receptivity, when telepathy actually works through a completely free and open state of mind.

One clear reflection we have upon the ground, of the increase in communications and thought transference across the globe, is through the computer Internet. This is a close physical reflection of how our collective mind works and interacts: the collective mind represents the data base and world wide web, a type of archives for the collective imprints of all thoughts, feelings, experiences and human lives to date. This is the central mainframe computer. From here all the individual minds can draw, interact with, and relate information and experience. They can communicate with each other, draw information from the past, view what is happening in the present, and they can even link with and work with a whole group of people at once, spread out across the globe.

The Internet is an interconnected web of communication lines, that enables people all over the world to link together, swap information and communicate, in just the same manner as the collective mind of humanity and the Universe as a whole. The only difference is the technological hardware needed to enter the internet, and the fact that any level of awareness can enter and use the web, regardless of the nature of their intentions. As the veil of the Abyss is continually dissolved and our spiritual subconscious becomes more exposed and consciously realised, so we will naturally become more directly telepathic. The knowledge within the collective mind will become more inherent and freely available, while individuals and groups of individuals will be able to remain in constant open contact and communication, regardless of where they are on the planet.

As our perspective of life moves on beyond the dominance of the physical, to centre around the eternal nature of the soul, so our fear of death will fade into the past. We will consciously be able to appreciate the transition through birth and death, as spirit passing into the physical realms of human nature and back out again. We will view the potential of life from the perspective of how our soul can evolve and become more enlightened. Communication and support between disincarnate and incarnate souls will become more natural and common to us; it will no longer be viewed as communication with the dead, but as communication with the ever-living souls of our spiritual family.

As human beings we will begin to open up and flower, we will become spiritual entities, channels for the light and energy of the Universe. As our personal desires will no longer have the dominance with which to distort and imbalance this channelling, so it will be able to pass through in complete harmony with nature, according to need and attraction. The Earth and everything upon it, animal, vegetable and mineral, will also be raised in its evolution by this influx of Universal energy. The higher awareness and energy that is filtered through the Earth's atmosphere and grounded by humans, will act as if to fine tune and perfect nature. Communications with animals and natural elements will develop, ecosystems will balance and flourish, violent instincts will be calmed and re-adapted, everything will come to shine of its fullest colour and potential. Like a perfected piece of art the Earth will open and offer its experience to the rest of the Universe.

Human societies will become completely co-operative and communal as we move into the future. We will all come to know our common origins and soul identity, overcoming the destructive thought patterns of prejudice and judgement. Whilst retaining our individuality and its unique path to enlightenment, our cultures will openly share and celebrate their diversity and colour as part of the abundant variety of Earth. Communities around the world will merge with and build within the Earth's nature, using natural and renewable resources and drawing energy direct from the Universe's infinite potential. They will become more self-sufficient, networking together and supporting each other, and they will interweave their social structures with the nature and knowledge drawn in from the rest of the Universe. Our reasons and needs for incarnating will change. Gone will be the old long karmic cycle towards self-realisation and enlightenment. The human focus and experience will almost completely move on to Universal knowledge, art and creativity, teaching the control, directing and manifestation of energy. This will offer the skills and experience that will prepare the human soul to eventually become the central opening and intelligence for new star systems and creations to come into being.

As the doors to the Universe open and our consciousness merges, so we will begin to discover and communicate with the abundance of other evolving life forms and beings that exist. The pathway will be open for us to incarnate and experience other natures, planets and star systems, and for souls that have evolved elsewhere to incarnate into human nature. Because of its physical nature and the diversity for expression and communication, the Earth has the potential to become a planet of conference within the Universe. Souls will be free to come and go as they need, and alien life forms and entities can share their knowledge and experience in exchange for that of the Earth and the human race. The experience of the Earth has a lot to offer the Universe. The resistance to our progressive evolution created by fear and greed, has meant that the human soul has had to draw upon greater strength and determination. This has led to increased diversity and individual expression, and has helped to bring forward numerous new ideas and concepts for creation to explore. In Scientific terms: the more resistance there is to a current or flow of energy, then the more energy is required to overcome the resistance and continue the flow; given that the potential source of energy is infinite, then more work is done and more potential is made real.

In the present day, as our transition in awareness takes place, so our minds are opened to thoughts and perceptions of alien life, and these are introduced and developed within our consciousness. Admittedly many of our perceptions are still dominated by our protective fearing animal instincts: the fear of invasion, being dominated, destroyed, enslaved, and the conspiracy theories of undercover invasion and manipulation. The thought of other beings in the Universe with far greater knowledge and technology, dissolves our notions of superiority and exposes our vulnerabilities. But these fearful projections as to the possible intents of alien beings, merely reflects back on us and our still primitive nature and naive view of the Universe.

Granted it is possible that beings more highly advanced and evolved could take over the planet and destroy or dominate our race, but if this were the case, then how could the Universe find any stability if hostile and destructive beings were free to roam and do as they pleased? This human perception of alien life merely exposes one of our own possible reactions to being in a position of superiority and power, for in reality, part of any soul's requirement in evolution to reaching a level of Universal enlightenment and freedom, is the relinquishing of self-interest for the interests of the collective. In this respect, any alien life forms that are involved in our evolution and transition, and are free to move within the Universe, have had to merge with its consciousness, and now exist to serve its evolving needs. They support, implement and direct whatever is taking place, according to need and attraction, thus always maintaining a balance of energy

Other evolved entities and life forms existed way before even the conception of the Earth. They have, I believe, played an important part in ours and the Earth's evolution from the very start and up to the present day. Guiding our direction, implementing new ideas, thought patterns and directives as they arise within the Universe, and drawing from our own experience to pass on new ideas to other creations. Such beings are not truly alien, they are no different from us in spirit, they have just evolved through different forms, experiences and planets, to become aware of and serve the nature of the Universe in their own unique ways. They are the hands, eyes and ears of the Universe, something we too have the potential to become as we realise our spiritual identity and Universal nature. They are only alien to us at present because they still remain within the darkness of the unknown and outside of our direct collective experience and awareness, and it is because of this that we regularly depict them in an ugly image that reflects our own fears and superstitions.

These primitive fears will continue to dissolve with the dominance of our animal instincts. In time, contact with aliens will become commonly accepted as part of everyday life. Their interactions may have a strong affect on the formation of our future societies: their knowledge and experiences of the Universe and their technologies, could help to advance our own evolution and awareness in a relatively short space of time. For the moment however, they will continue to remain on the outskirts of our consciousness, giving us the occasional sign of their presence, so as to stimulate our curiosity and help to bring out our fears. They could not reveal themselves directly today, for the simple reason that this might interfere with our present evolution and transition (affecting our freedom of choice), and expose too much fear too quickly. We are learning to trust and follow our soul instincts above our self-preserving fears, free from outside interference and inducement, and the direct collective exposure of alien entities and their Universal awareness would, in our present position, greatly influence this transition. Aliens have no impulse to even contemplate interfering, they have an over-view or our collective evolution and its needs, and they are well aware of the possible anxiety, fear and chaos that would be the immediate reaction to their revealing themselves.

Having said that, we are in the present being gradually introduced to and prepared for real contact with alien beings; the signs and symptoms are all around us. I have little respect for or interest in conspiracy theories, simply because they have no ultimate power to dictate our direction in thinking and evolution. Most tend to accredit manipulative government agencies with far more intelligence than they actually posses. Most conspiracy theories have been concocted and used to create the illusion of knowing more than we actually do, and most are now the remnants of outdated tools for war propaganda, used to induce fear and demand respect ('we know something that you don't'). Alien beings seek the open minds of loving, enlightened human souls as their bridge to communication and exposure, regardless of their status within society or government.

Some of us today, whether conscious of it or not, may be souls that have evolved within other star systems, helping this transition upon the ground; remember they are as human as the next soul once they have entered into human genetics. It is such open minds as these that are helping to expose the possibilities of positive contact with other forms of life; not necessarily alien, but different, as of yet unknown. These concepts are entering into our individual minds and everyday lives, expressed through the popular media of films, books and television (directly alongside the more fearful perceptions of alien beings, that are helping to expose and release these fears). Believe or disbelieve, it matters little: 100 years ago few people even considered the concept of aliens, where as now few people fail to have an opinion about them. In God's good time we shall be exposed to the truth...

And so these are just a few of my projections into the future; general ideas and themes that are already visible within our race, that will one day come to be fully exposed and realised. I personally do not know when, but I do know that we are one step closer with every passing day. And it is here in the present that I look to remain, for this is the path that leads to the future and enables our potential to become a living reality. As far as I'm concerned the 'when' is when we are ready, when we have faced and learnt what we need to evolve. Your immediate future is in your hands, the place where it has always been....

Part 3

Self-discovery

Self-discovery

The final part of this book is a progressive collection of thoughts and feelings that go some way to expressing my own personal experiences of self-discovery and awakening. I began writing as a teenager, seventeen years ago. I had recently given up studying at University, but more than this, I gave up a whole preconceived direction in life, a path that was already laid out before me. My only justification to those that knew me, was that it did not feel alive or hold any real inspiration. What was to come next I had no idea. I had made my first completely independent and honest decision about life and basically started again from scratch, thinking about the world and contemplating life from an honest and fairly detached perspective.

I had no previous inclination towards writing. I was a fairly naive teenager who had read very little and who had never really travelled much; I stood alone without any real care or direction in life. My only heart felt instinct was an inner determination that whatever path I walked and created, and whatever words I spoke, would be completely honest with what I felt about life inside. I had no desire to look for other peoples answers, just an inner curiosity to know, and I made a simple commitment to follow that instinct above all else, even if it led to my death. From there, with an open mind, thoughts and feelings came flooding through naturally: they would carry me away from the world, breaking down old thought patterns and judgements that I had been raised and educated with, and revealing a new perspective that to me was completely original and heart felt. At times I would scramble to write things down, returning from this drifting experience to go back into the world and to earn the money I needed to live. Feelings would almost express themselves in words, with little effort on my part, and I would use them to re-connect with my previous train of thought, once the work of earning a living had been taken care of. Hence the need and inspiration for writing was born within me.

I still have read fairly little and I have not physically done much travelling, but I do not believe these things are essential to gaining knowledge. They can facilitate your experience of yourself and give you a more direct experience of the present ways of this world we live in, but I believe all true knowledge comes simply through an open mind, wherever you may be. This is how the Universe reveals itself to us, and thus how we come to see the truth in the world around us. While I have since discovered similar writings and thoughts to my own, everything you have read here came from the real experience and inspiration of my own self-discovery. It bred a feeling of being totally alive that would leave me no doubts as to its authenticity. I realise that this is a most personal expression of feelings and opinions, and I only offer them in the hope that they might help to stimulate others thoughts and self-discovery.

At the end of this process of my own self-discovery, upon which I felt completely drawn and carried by the Universe, I experienced a period of profound realisation and awakening: an energy and emotion that words could not describe. It was completely overwhelming and unexpected, all embracing, enlightening and most beautiful. My feet were lifted from the ground (although not literally), my heart was blown wide open and it felt as if the energy of the Universe was flooding through my entire being. Everything I looked and thought upon seemed to reveal itself instantly; as I embraced it, I connected with and became the nature of everything around me.

This overpowering flow of energy gradually elapsed and calmed over a period of weeks and months. On a personal note it had revealed to me the realities of previous lives (something I had not previously contemplated), and it was as if the experience of these lives subtly integrated with my present personality and consciousness. Souls that I had spent time with in previous lives were revealed as friends I had within the present, and people I was yet to meet. From that time forwards I have trusted the instincts of my heart completely. They have revealed just enough to keep me moving in the desired directions. Often I have no idea as to what comes next, but it always fits into place once it has arrived, or I have entered into it. Opportunities have been taken up, karma has been resolved, and ties have been released, all helping to support the transition underway within our collective consciousness.

In recent years my feet have become grounded again to walk in our day-to-day reality, and I have gathered the words to translate this overwhelming connection and experience, and present them as you now read. Language will always have its limitations; these are the best words that I have come to find, for now, to express my own personal experience of life within the Universe. Call it a revelation from God..., a prophecy..., a basis for new integrated science (which includes the immeasurable experience and consciousness of the spirit and soul)..., call it the delusions of wishful thinking..., or just the ramblings of a madman... To me it is my natural perception and experience of life, and nothing can ever take that away.

I am just an ordinary human being, I certainly do not lay claim to having all the answers, but I do claim to have found all these answers for myself; something that we are all free to do. I still have plenty to learn from this present life on Earth, and hopefully plenty more to give, and I believe that all the answers you need to learn from are there, just waiting to reveal themselves. I will continue to walk forward into the future, as always, with an open mind. Here now is the voice of my soul, translated from the pure thoughts and feelings of a direct contact with the spirit and consciousness of God, into the words that you now read..... Thank you for your time, and may your own journey ahead always lead you where you need to go.

*As I lay upon the Earth and close my eyes,
so this body returns to dust, to release me from my
physical ties:
it is then that the spirits speak their tongue;
calling me back, to the essence of our original
purpose.
I lay upon the shore:
like waves their whispers calmly wash through my
soul;
and when this drift is returned to land,
the spirit shines pure, once more upon the Earth;
enlightened by the truth....*

*The time has come at last to set the sail;
to embrace the one eternal source:
I know not where it leads me,
nor where I shall find an end;
but I give up all that is my life,
to fulfil this final quest....*

*****

When the son decides to take full responsibility for his life,
then it is time to walk the way alone:
and when this path has found its destination;
so the son now becomes the father.

*****

In our submission to the spirit,
that cries out from deep within;
then we are brought deliverance,
from all this worldly pain:

born into the outside;
every bond exposed through honest sight,
releases hold to give forth its wisdom,
and return you to the heart;

and at the very centre,
lies our final rest:
the knowledge of silent wisdom,
eternally reborn....

*****

The images of self-expression that we create upon the surface,
are not always honest with that which lies beneath:
civilisation is the clothes that we choose to hide behind;
for underneath us all, there lies the naked truth.

*****

Words are nothing without feeling:
as I write these words they feel like everything to me;
but if I should return to these words, and give nothing to them;
to see just a piece of literature before my eyes;
then again these words are nothing:
If you were to read in such a way,
then nothing would be shared between us...

*****

*To be meek in the eyes of all nations and peoples,
is to be free of the need to uphold the ego;
to be humble in the face of their anger and hatred,
is to share the most simple enlightenment, of love...*

*****

*To ponder on regret,
is to follow the path that leads away from the living:
the desire for a second chance has killed many before their time.
There is no second chance within the past;
every experience, whether judged right or wrong in consequence,
belongs to you:
look on it as such,
and you may begin to appreciate all that life can teach.*

*****

*There is so much today to fill the mind;
filling the mind, and yet leaving it unfulfilled...*

*****

*Do not let an honest thought or questioning pass
you by;
listen to this instinct:
this is what you are;
do not ignore what it tells you,
to trade your self-discovery
and hide in the knowledge of those that went
before:
nurture the seeds of your own mind;
allow the truth to grow.*

*****

This life that passes, is all a mere experience:
the fluctuations of emotion, and the changes of time;
to stand back in fear, then we may be cut by emotion,
and the memory in these scars, become the sculpture of our fate;
but if we should step through fear, to question and explore,
then the chisel is brought within our grasp:
and when all fear has been chipped away,
then the discovery of truth shall remain for ever,
in the most indestructible of statures,
emanating unconditional love...

*****

*From the beginning today,
then we are told what is evil and wrong,
and made to fear this, through superstition and
punishment;
and we are told what is good and right,
and made to emulate this, through praise and
reward:
the decisions were made for us:
but the strength of fear and desire would grow as
we did,
and they cannot leave until we decide for
ourselves.*

*The way to learning needs to be left open and
independent,
if we are ever to be free:
no force outside of ourselves,
no laws outside of our nature,
and no influence of possessive overbearance....
just the simple guidance to find the answers
within ourselves.*

*****

*Were these forces of hatred, anger and greed,
induced by our own desire for more...
or have they always been part of our fate in life:*

*The nature of an animal is selfish:
to preserve and survive,
then the first allegiance must be to the self.*

*****

*Mankind has become so proud of its race;
everything we consider to have life,
is looked down upon in comparison to man;
and yet man can seem so insignificant
through the eye's of nature;
snapped like a twig underfoot...*

*Man has not yet learned the responsibility
to preserve as a race;
which needs its natural environment to survive;
and so we fight to create our own laws...;
evolution will continue,
long after we are extinct....*

*****

What we allow to possess our mind,
will then become our conscious reality:
Once the physical body that we live through,
is understood as part of nature that shall pass,
and not as ours to keep,
then we will no longer be dominated,
by its many pleasures and pains:
its limits will cease to be our struggle,
and its substance, our primitive reality:
from here we begin to reach the higher ground

*****

The peoples of the world:
they feel for each other, they fend for each other,
they give to each other, they love each other...;
still, at times, they are blinded in each other's
company:
they ignore each other, they fight each other,
they kill each other, they do not know each
other...;
and so many times comes the feeling,
that we have realised our mistakes too late...

*****

One action of ignorance can poison the mind:
until it is given its time of repentance,
to accept the antidote of understanding;
then there can be no real peace of mind.

*****

A just word needs no justification,
it will always speak for itself...

*****

Violent passion is nature's law to many animals;
for us to lose such base desires,
is to find the way to peace:
calm the many tides of desire,
that swell towards unbridled passion,
for this alone shall set the spirit free.

Our animal instincts tie us with a sometimes savage past;
if we allow them to dictate, we may be taken;
but if there is to be an awakening,
then there is much to learn in the conquering of such instincts.

*****

Hope can be painful:
so many people today,
who have not become engulfed in selfishness,
or overcome by despair, to be cynical,
live their lives through hope;
but still they remain in hiding,
too fearful to fulfil their hope:
hope can be painful.

*****

To fight what you know to be wrong, will not rid you
of it,
you must take no further part to lose its hold.

*****

God's Calling

While so many heads are down,
Inspiration will always be too rare;
So few allow to give themselves up,
To its racing passion and overwhelming embrace;
And we all should run with such powerful rivers,
For they lead to the open sea,
That is the fullness of our life....
If you are to withhold and ignore;
Obstructing a dam before the new flowing river:
Its meaning cut off to the sea...,
Its energy drained elsewhere...,
Then life is starved of its experience.

The face of inspiration is unmistakable,
It belongs to you:
Fixated eyes - the rapids are upon us;
In panic you may cough and splutter to shore,
but you owe to be taken by such currents,
For they are both our source and fulfilment:
The flow is vigorous and swelling,
The stomach flutters - the heart pounds - beats quicken,
Senses are primed - mind is strong and determined,
Head raised in recognition....
INSPIRATION!!!

We may never come to sail our sea
If its source is continually diverted:
Flow all rivers and join all Oceans,
So water may flood the world once more;
That we may be purified and enlightened,
By divine inspiration.....

*****

*It is only by confronting our fears,
that we may truly begin to learn what lies
beyond.*

*****

*We must always look to ourselves to gain
freedom:
if there were one word that could give us
understanding,
then we spread this word, so that all may
understand:
but this could never work in practice,
as language is communal for one reason only:
that of mutual understanding;
so if we were to speak this word,
to one who has not discovered it for themselves,
then they would not be able to truly understand.
And so we must all find our own answers,
To know the truth of self discovery.*

*****

Continually they search for the scientific solution,
and yet we ourselves made such science up:
there will always be a problem, in the search for a solution;
some of our answers lie in our simple acceptance:
there is no solution to that which is eternal....
it just is

*****

I flowed in the dreams of discovery
and I was most content alone
To offer this is futile
if another is to feel such freedom
then they to must be alone
and there it is that we shall come together

*****

Security will come, not to those who hold on,
but to those who can let go.

*****

Pride can force you to take a stand,
and you must fight to keep its glory:
life can be ignorant, with pride at hand;
and when yours is lost, here ends the story.

*****

Can you see through death, without the fear...?
It lies peacefully, with assurance...

*****

Do you see the miracle in life..?
Then you will know that nothing is impossible...

*****

Dreaming of Reality

I am up high, alone;
beholding the beauty of evolution,
in the pure green forest that stretches out before me,
reaching beyond the sight of my eyes;
the only comparison to such immense nature,
is the hazy sky above, looking on in awe,
as I myself am struck:
nothing could harm this,
nor would anything desire so, if it had such sight:
so vast, could any know of all its secrets;
yet I feel intimate with every tiny detail:
I sensed the radiant life,
and in this there was no doubt.

I returned like a sapling, once more into the ground:
edging the forest, I saw the blindness of our ignorance,
surrounded by man, desperate to feed his progress:
I watched the trees falling one by one,
while workers sparked and joked about their lives;
I could not talk:
as my voice remained silent, I felt the pain of every weeping stump,
left to mark the grave of the beauty that was:
it is not only the trees,
but also a part of ourselves that we destroy:
I sensed the darkness of death,
trampling everything within its fearful reach.

I left this place to reach still higher in my hopes:
alone again, I studied the human race,
stumbling, as they searched impatiently below:
I was overcome by the possibilities of love,
that they seemed to neglect in their rush;
the need of which wept away in every heart:
everyone was different in sight, and separate to touch,
but from here I could see them only as one:
I sensed the radiant life,
and again there was no doubt.

Feeling rejuvenated, I returned from this distant vision,
but no more could I see the people together:
from the same spring their beliefs had flown,
only now they allied with pride,
and were quick to provoke the emotions of a fighting passion:
this forced men and women apart,
into more and more divided nations;
each with self righteousness as their cause,
and few ready to compromise:
they were happy to play games,
that with one wrong move, could slaughter innocent lives:
I sensed the ignorance of death,
indifferent to its victims.

With this I felt I could stay no more;
banished from this world by the honesty of what I saw:
it was then that eternity had me cradled:
it showed me everything to be as one;
casting no judgement, nor moving to either side;

I lay in peace, completely undisturbed,
wandering through all pasts, and possible futures:
'they would always change', it said to me,
'but I shall always be...':
here I now sensed life and death together:
no beginning, and no end...,
no doubt, and no fear....

*****

I now touch death..., engulfed by peace;
this body will not be taken by time:
in this death the soul finds freedom from the body,
their separation no longer being forced.

*****

Love is not the spoken word...,
but the voicing of a soul.

*****

Christmas Day 1989

It was a day of celebration,
for this loving man, sadly now forgotten;
rarely a moments thought passed his way, but to
clear a conscience.
I walked alone;
the littering waste of our empty lives swirled
about the streets;
a sandstorm of societies desert,
that blew deep into the heart,
and flooded my mind with despair.

Then my eyes were moved by the figure of a man;
as he approached he was ignorant of my presence
to the last:
head down he swayed and stumbled,
his feet no longer directed by thought or care,
but by any intoxicating liquid he could lay his
hands on:
all about him said that he had lost all hope for his
own life,
and now pitifully drank away the haunting
future,
of the many that could not see.
As he drew alongside, his heavy head rose from its
slumber,
and his drunken eyes came to meet my own:
In that instant we came together:
many eyes I have studied in my time,
mostly selfish, unfulfilled and unmoving;
but as our visions locked together, pupil to
teacher,
I have never learnt nor felt so much,
as the intensity of his gaze inspired:

It told me of his life:
how his heart had been broken by the cruelty of
this world;
and central to this lay his prophecy,
of a society that would be forced to remember,
due to the ignorance of their ways.
This living philosopher needed no pen or tongue to
speak;
he was wise in not wasting words of wisdom,
on those too deaf even to hear his begging...

For that brief moment his eyes widened and he
came alive;
in my youth was his rebirth:
our souls exchanged and danced,
as he knew I understood,
and in the flicker of an eye he lived a whole new
life....
But as his head was spinning, his years spent,
and his heart corroded by wine,
his gaze quickly collapsed,
and our meeting was ended:
head sinking, he stumbled on,
just as he had arrived.

Hope had not the strength to save him before,
and would not do so now;
but as for me:
he had established a will impenetrable by time's
weary ways:
whereas before despair may have taken my days
also,
now, through him, I had seen its course before its
time,

and I was eternally stronger inside;
hope would not die in my eyes;
in this life I would live to see some truth
resurrected...
And to him, who I, if no one else, will remember,
I now give these words back:
that his life was not in vain to be washed away:
for on this day I found salvation.

*****

Compassion will teach;
but if it were to be my only teacher,
then today's world would carry me away,
and destroy me in its cruelty.

*****

In selfishness, then we only deny ourselves:
for eventually we cut off the hand that feeds us with
life.

*****

In the story of our world today,
then we are all the authors:
we each dictate our own chapter,
and we all have the power to write the truth...

*****

All the writers of philosophy seemed so certain of their theories;
all the readers of these, are still so,
merely to continue the question...:
and the simple truth carries us on regardless.

*****

I reach out from these words,
to offer you eternity:
it is never mine to give,
but always yours to know...

*****

Two men face their own deaths:
The first gasps for life, as he breaths his final air;
his eyes are drowned in panic;
his hand out-stretched, crippled with a quaking fear,
as he exposes the futile struggle to hold on.....
The second lies motionless, with eyes wide and welcoming;
he breaths in deep, towards a peaceful end:
all his life is behind him now,
and he is free, just as he has always been;
now, as he lets go, he understands why....

Both are laid to rest,
but only the memory of one shall rest in peace.

*****

A will that merely stands against the beliefs of others,
reflects an emptiness within itself;
A will that shows the strength to follow its own beliefs,
will, in time, find a way to fulfilment.

*****

*To accept the word of another,
in answer to your own questioning,
will always leave you obligated.*

*****

*The ugly face of arrogance,
is a play to mask the fear,
that those who desire power choose to wear:
it is time to remove those masks and reveal the truth...*

*****

<u>The resurrection of faith</u>

*Three days of fear it took to see,
that such pure faith could never die:
a man may lose his body in many ways,
but if his life upheld a faith, so true and sincere,
then nothing is ever taken or changed by his death:
he shall remain always, to live on as love.*

*****

Words can be such poor testimony to faith:
while they may be spoken or written,
in moments of sincerity,
if they are not lived,
then sincerity is lost.

*****

Mourning is compassion to the extreme:
a life has passed that you once shared,
and now you must share in its death...;
but from this confrontation,
you can find such strength and know such truth;
for death tells no lies and can never be deceived:
this, through compassion, is yours to see;
now again you must move on alone.

*****

Meditation: to be one with all consciousness...

*****

Wisdom is the word of truth, we each must find for ourselves.

*****

Any hardship in life,
is that which goes against our selfish will,
all of our own making:
if we can only give up this will,
then this is the way to God.

*****

Jesus to all followers

Through the faith I have lived in this life,
and spoken of through these words;
then you may touch that faith through me:
but I am only such an opening,
that you may come to know this faith for
yourself.
I am not to be the bearer of your faith;
in finding God alone, then you shall find me,
and all others who rest in peace.
I have become that peace we all seek for ourselves;
you must not follow me to fulfil your quest;
there is never an end for one who merely follows
another;
when your leader is gone, you will find yourself
lost once more;
you must all find leadership within yourselves,
and from there make your own way forward.

*****

We all must have faith, to step into the darkness,
before we may see the light.

*****

To know that which is eternal,
you must be ready to give up everything
that is temporal about your being.

*****

A temporary hell may lead us to heaven,
when such a past is ready to die.

*****

Walk not blindly upon your chosen path,
but with faith in your heart that spirit shall guide,
and should you step into joy or pain,
except all openly,
for these are your honest needs.

*****

*Everything is relative within the limits we perceive;
if we were to know eternity,
there would be no comparison.*

*****

*The word of God:
it is etched in every soul,
only viewed within:
God remains elated in its rarity,
as few look to themselves for this word.*

*****

*In the verdict of every judgement, we pronounce our own sentence:
for it is thus that our minds are opened and closed.*

*****

To be vague with words,
is not necessarily to be unimaginative,
but to leave more to the imagination of others...

*****

It is only what you have considered in yourself,
that you may truly come to recognise in others...

*****

Compromise to your faith:
take no part in it,
for it may take part of you.

*****

This is the voice of my soul;
these are its teachings to me;
these are the words of my own self-discovery;
now that my eyes are open,
I can return to the world.

Second Coming

Before I came this time,
I was immersed......:
a stream in the infinite ocean,
one with everything;
the emanation of spirit disembodied,
carried in the tide of every flowering creation;
ecstatic by the chorus of harmonious stars
majestic unfolding...:
this was heaven...

But the time had come:
the Earth and its children cried out for fulfilment,
and I was drawn in to return once again;
it was always a part of me to see this complete:
the seed had been sown many centuries ago,
germinated by the blood of continual self
sacrifice;
now the fruit burst, ready for the harvest...

By decree the portal from heaven was opened,
guiding me down through the influxing vortex;
a path was prepared to walk upon the shore,
interlocked with the key God's grace had
bestowed;
I entered...., borne of the ocean;
delivered through the human seed;
so began this present incarnation:

As a child I was to forget;
mind re-embracing the gift of our nature,
for I knew the joy of this place to be Earth......,
and yet, in time the tide of memory turns back,

and I awake to the message within these very words:
"Christ comes as the wave of God's infinite Ocean,
breaking over the Earth..., flooding us all...;
all fear is exposed, all resistance broken,
till peace is inherent, and fulfilment known...:
so shall this be..., Heaven on Earth."

Remember these words in the years that follow:
the waiting is over..., the time is now...,
the harvest has begun...

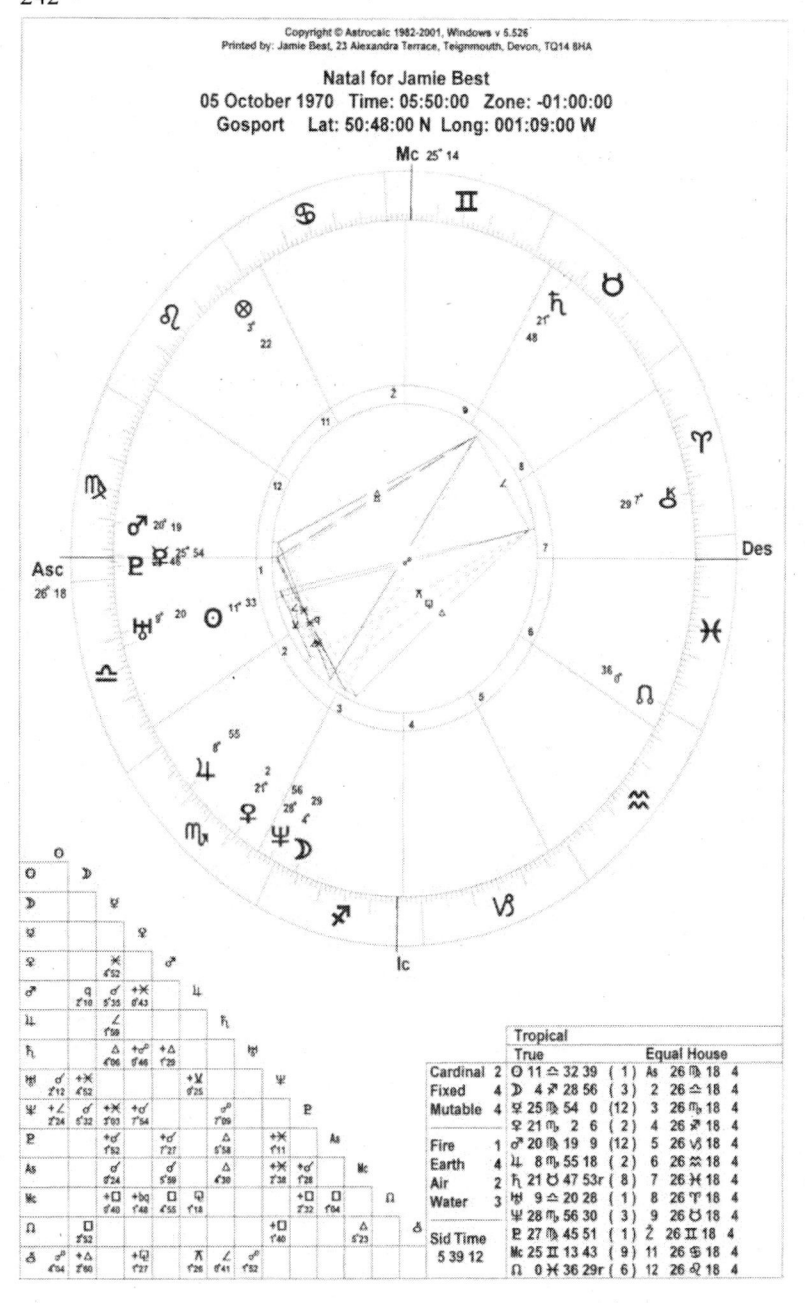

Natal for Jamie Best
05 October 1970 Time: 05:50:00 Zone: -01:00:00
Gosport Lat: 50:48:00 N Long: 001:09:00 W

Jamie Best is always interested in your comments and questions regarding these ideas and life in general. He can be contacted at:

jbest1970@yahoo.co.uk

or

23, Alexandra Terrace,
Teignmouth,
Devon,
United Kingdom
TQ14 8HA

ISBN 142512963-3